Ex Captivitate Salus

Ex Captivitate Salus
Experiences, 1945–47

Carl Schmitt

Edited by Andreas Kalyvas
and Federico Finchelstein

Translated by Matthew Hannah

polity

First published in German as *Ex Captivitate Salus. Erfahrungen der Zeit 1945/47*, by Greven Verlag, Cologne, 1950. Fourth, extended edition © Duncker & Humblot GmbH, Berlin, 2015.

This English edition © Polity Press, 2017

Polity Press
65 Bridge Street
Cambridge CB2 1UR, UK

Polity Press
101 Station Landing, Suite 300
Medford, MA 02155, USA

ISBN-13: 978-1-5095-1163-1
ISBN-13: 978-1-5095-1164-8 (pb)

A catalogue record for this book is available from the British Library.
Names: Schmitt, Carl, 1888-1985, author.
Title: Ex captivitate salus : experiences, 1945-47 / Carl Schmitt.
Other titles: Ex captivitate salus. English.
Description: Cambridge, UK ; Malden, MA, USA : Polity Press, 2017. | Includes bibliographical references and index.
Identifiers: LCCN 2017010109 (print) | LCCN 2017031142 (ebook) | ISBN 9781509511662 (Mobi) | ISBN 9781509511679 (Epub) | ISBN 9781509511631 (hardback) | ISBN 9781509511648 (pbk.)
Subjects: LCSH: Schmitt, Carl, 1888-1985. | Law--Philosophy. | Law teachers--Germany--Biography. | Nazis--Germany--Biography. | Prisoners' writings, German.
Classification: LCC K230.S352 (ebook) | LCC K230.S352 E3313 2017 (print) | DDC 340.092--dc23
LC record available at https://lccn.loc.gov/2017010109

Typeset in 11 on 14 pt Adobe Caslon by Servis Filmsetting Ltd, Stockport, Cheshire
Printed and bound in the United Kingdom by Clays Ltd, St Ives PLC

For further information on Polity, visit our website: politybooks.com

IN MEMORIAM
DR. WILHELM AHLMANN
† December 7, 1944

CÆCUS DEO PROPIVS

Contents

Translator's Note

All translator interventions appear in square brackets, either in the main text or in footnotes. Most of Schmitt's gendered pronouns are left as in the original, in part because he often clearly had himself in mind when writing of anonymous individuals. "Humankind," "humanity" and related terms are, however, substituted for "man" or "men" where this does not detract from the resulting English. The translator would like to acknowledge the assistance of George Schwab, the virtuoso copy-editing of Manuela Tecusan, the comments and suggestions of Andreas Kalyvas, Federico Finchelstein and Rory Rowan, and the supportive guidance of Paul Young.

Introduction

Carl Schmitt's Prison Writings

Andreas Kalyvas and Federico Finchelstein

I am naked.

Carl Schmitt[1]

If 1945 was a turning point in world history, it was especially
so for Carl Schmitt's intellectual, academic, public, and personal trajectory. Global reality had changed in unexpected
ways: from a world disputed by three ideologies—fascism,
communism, and liberalism—to a post-European Cold War
between the last two, which had allied and defeated the
first. Undoubtedly Schmitt was considered one of the most
prominent intellectuals in the defeated camp. An admirer
of Mussolini's fascist dictatorship, an ambitious member
of the Nazi Party—which he joined on the same day as
Martin Heidegger, just a few months after Adolf Hitler
came to power in January 1933—and a vocal anti-Semite
thereafter, Schmitt had seriously contemplated the prospect
of becoming a leading voice in national socialist theory.[2] He
wanted to determine its content and decide its direction.[3]
He was perceived at the time as the "crown jurist of the
Third Reich," someone who sought to endow the regime
with a new legal theory of politics and all the reputation and

legitimacy consequent upon it.[4] It was a theory he tailored to fit the Führer's aspirations to become the only source of legality.[5]

To be sure, Schmitt's work cannot be reduced to his Nazi period. Ultimately, as it became evident in 1936, it was not as influential with the Nazis as he had wanted it to be. But at the same time it cannot be disconnected from Nazism. Before 1933 he authored seminal works on political theology, dictatorship and the state of emergency, political myth, sovereignty, constitutionalism, and, most importantly, enmity as the defining element of the political. After 1933 he sought to recalibrate his work in the direction of international law and world politics, so as to fit the ideological imperatives of the Nazis and avoid party suspicions. However, what defined Schmitt all along and informed his theoretical explorations was his fierce opposition to liberalism and communism. In the new bipolar world that emerged after the fall of Berlin, his long-standing enemies had won and were in a unique position to determine the new political landscape. As fascism was defeated and his enemies victorious, Schmitt had to rethink himself, his work, and his own political standing and, as his biographer Reinhard Mehring put it, to "attempt to establish one's identity in the battle for recognition."[6]

* * *

This battle was conducted from prison. Schmitt was arrested twice in 1945 and stripped of his prestigious professorship in Berlin, his library was confiscated, and he spent more than one year in two civilian detention camps, being incarcerated and interrogated again by the Allies, in the spring of 1947, at Nuremberg. At the dawn of a new era that seemingly had no space for him, he found himself out of place, defeated, and "naked"—a victim unjustly persecuted, "weak" and "defense-less" inside a cell.[7] This was the abrupt context in which he secretly wrote this book and which Jacob Taubes, professor of Jewish studies at the Free University of Berlin and Schmitt's postwar interlocutor, has described as Schmitt's "broken confessions."[8]

In prison Schmitt, who was designated by the allies in 1947 as a "potential defendant" in war crimes, dedicated most of his time to vindicate his past, his work, and himself against charges that in one way or another made him complicit in and responsible for the crimes of Nazism.[9] His prison writings therefore consist of a kind of judicial rhetoric that aims to vindicate its author, staging a public self-defense against wrongful accusations. Suitably, they start on a defensive tone, with Schmitt's reaction to the German philosopher and pedagogue Eduard Spranger's "unfathomable" and (in Schmitt's eyes) improper question: "Who are you?" This question, which Schmitt sees as a reproach and a provocation, hence implicitly as "a serious accusation," sets the stage for his response in the form of a self-defense but also offers him a reason to plan a philosophical and political intervention.[10] It compels him to compose the most intimate of his books.[11] "I have spoken of myself here," he claims, "actually for the first time in my life."[12] Although Schmitt rejected the confessional and apologetic tone of prison prose literature and in general questioned the ideal of self-transparency, he becomes for the first and last time his own main topic, his own object of inquiry from the beginning to the end of the book. Neither before nor after this text did he put himself in this self-reflective visible subject position. In his weakest moment Schmitt attempts to reach his readers through a most personal tone, allowing them to see the author behind the work, the person and not the party member, a professor and a scholar instead of a fanatic ideologue. Never again will he resort to so many self-descriptions, comparisons, analogies, and associations, all centered upon himself. The prison writings are a passionate attempt to repress his writings from the national socialist period, reinvent himself, and rebuild his damaged reputation. This is why this book represents such an evocative and unique statement of Schmitt's own self-understanding.[13]

To be sure, there are a few other postwar texts by him that could be considered personal in some way. For instance, in his dialogues on power and space in the 1950s, Schmitt will stage himself as an interlocutor among some fictional characters.[14] But in these brief dialogues he still emerges in a mediated form, like a character in a play. By contrast, in the prison writings he speaks directly to the readers, assuming responsibility for his own voice and thus attempting to bypass the narrative limits of representation. In a sense, he wanted this little book to stand directly for his own experience, for his own self. And unlike his private diaries, the writings from the cell were deliberatively composed for an immediate public. Schmitt clearly expected that there was a sympathetic audience out there, open to the unapologetic perspective of a former member of the Nazi Party. Although he conceived of his readership very selectively and in intimate terms, he also wrote for all those who were acquainted with his previous work and aware of his Nazi period, but who could also empathize with his trajectory and potentially become receptive to his pleas. In fact, in the context of a total antifascist victory, this was a text that sought to reach out not only to those who had been defeated in the war but to a much broader audience of bystanders who could rehabilitate Schmitt's reputation and legacy.

While Schmitt was defeated—defeated as a German, as a jurist, as a European, and as a fascist—as a scholar he stated that he was "in no sense destroyed."[15] He felt he only needed to mount a satisfactory defense and provide an explanation for the role he played in the Third Reich. And he did so in this book. He took this task upon himself and offered his own political explanation in terms of a general theory of obedience that addresses the borderline case of resistance to tyranny by recasting the distinction between norm and exception from two new angles. In the prison writings Schmitt focused again on the exception, a core concept that defined his Weimar work, but this time he began from below, in the concrete context of civil war. Thus, surprisingly, he revisited the state of exception not from the theological heights of a sovereign power that decides to suspend normal order, as he had depicted it in his interwar years, but from the borderline position of a victim of civil war. Strikingly, he now construed his notion of power from the assumed position of the subordinate, the disenfranchised, the outlawed, the excluded, and the rightless.

These figures of exclusion represent extreme situations, Schmitt claimed. They are the new forms of enmity produced in this new age by the criminalization and dehumanization of the enemy. The post-Eurocentric enemy appears in lawless and violent spaces—spaces that confront the citizen with the unpredictable terror unleashed by civil war. In these anomalous and abnormal moments, he explained, the loyal citizen is caught in a situation that is both treacherous and hostile. Confronting a fratricidal battle, he faces the ultimate political question: he "must determine the boundaries of his loyalty himself," decide whether, when, and how to exchange submission for protection.[16] The decision to suspend or discontinue obedience reverts back to individual citizens and their judgment, because they are the ones who have to decide whether the state, especially a totalitarian state, a tyranny, is worse than civil war and the total war of all against all. As in his theory, in his own particular case Schmitt resolved this dilemma by questioning the rationality and expediency of disobedience and by choosing the tyrant over the natural state. The power asymmetry between a totalitarian one-party system and the individual, he said, is so great that resistance becomes impossible and the dissenter is ultimately thrown back into "the claws of the Leviathan itself."[17] Any order is better than disorder.[18] This line of argument became a belated justification of his membership of the Nazi Party and of his activities for and within Hitler's regime. As he explains in this book, accommodation with Nazism was therefore an existential necessity, a lesser evil, and a prudential act of survival under totalitarian domination. He said that victims of such extreme situations, such as himself, resembled closely Herman Melville's fictional character of Benito Cereno and his tragic adventures. They also evoked the enigmatic figure of a Christian Epimetheus and his Pandora's box.

Schmitt's first identification is with a literary character, a victim of deception, violence, and impotence who is taken captive and acts against his will, while the second is with a Christianized Greek mythical figure and his tragic, unintended error, provoked by manipulation but carried out by desire and love. Both figures, the literary and the mythical, are summoned up in the broader context set by the questions of personal responsibility and moral accountability, which are central to the structure of this book. These symbols are complex figures, polysemic and indefinable, and in Schmitt's writings they can betray a sense a grandeur that is oblivious to other important meanings: oppression, race and gender, and iniquity. But, for Schmitt, this double self-identification as Benito Cereno and the Christian Epimetheus is also his way of answering Spranger's initial question: "Who are you?"

Another striking dimension of the prison writings is how Schmitt regarded them as a portal to a deeper existential, historical, and political truth. This was the "wisdom of the cell." Thus, while his challenging personal situation was as wretched as he perceived it, he also treated it as offering him a privileged epistemic position. He conceived of his imprisonment as providing a space of solitary illumination, an objective standpoint—to both himself and the globe. It is not only that his experience of internment and interrogation and his overall construction of it through the trope of suffering achieve his desired outcome of personal redemption. There is more to it than that. Clearly Schmitt understood his internment as a form of political persecution and, more generally, as a concrete symptom of the spatial disorder, global civil wars, and international anomy he was describing and denouncing in his more academic writings.[19] The act of observation was now mediated and amplified by what he thought was an actual manifestation of the criminalization of war and the dehumanization of the enemy, two processes immanent in the revival of the just war doctrine that had occurred in the aftermath of the collapse of the European international order. "For in some respects," he claimed, "the kind of civil war carried out in the confessional wars of the sixteenth and seventeenth centuries in Europe and on colonial soil is repeating itself."[20] He thus appears as the paradigmatic victim of this collapse and of the ruins it left behind.

From such a standpoint he thought that he could see things better than the rest. For Schmitt, the act of witnessing defeat in civil war from his cell meant adopting an overpowering position vis-à-vis those who were not in prison. The cell gave him almost a monopoly of knowledge. As he asserted, "I am today… the only teacher of law on this earth who has recorded and experienced the problem of just war, including unfortunately civil war, in all of its depth and causes."[21] This certainty of being the subject who knows, "the last knowing representative of *ius publicum Europaeum*," led him to articulate a view that could in principle represent all those who—victims of civil war, like him—were without guilt, and even unfairly treated.[22] In short, he saw the imprisonment as a way to illuminate himself, his changing times, Germany, and Europe.

Schmitt's prison writings present a counternarrative to the narrative of the war victors, and this fact is echoed in his counterquestion to Spranger. He turns the question "Who are you?" against his various interrogators. He acknowledges that history is generally written by those who win; and he sets his carceral reflections against the dominant discourse that was emerging in the postwar context of the Bonn republic. Without even mentioning the massive war crimes that later came to define the Holocaust and to mark its history, Schmitt complains about the circumstances of the allied occupation, which he depicts as characterized by "concentrations camps," "deprivation of rights," and "mass internments" in which Americans and Russians had "defamed entire categories of the German population."[23] In 1958 he wrote, in the prologue to the Spanish edition of this book: "I was in such a camp under automatic arrest in 1945/6."[24] As a witness, he saw no logic to the juridical proceedings against Nazism and even denounced them as "the logical result of the criminalization of an entire people and the completion of the infamous Morgenthau Plan."[25] In this picture, where bystanders and perpetrators were turned into victims, there was no place for the real victims of the war. He characterized the famous Nuremberg judicial process as fully devoid of justice. He represented the postwar trials and his personal interment and interrogation as the result of the world-historical shift to the just war doctrine, its return and reinvention in the humanitarian campaigns waged by the United States and its allies. He says instead very little about the Nazi dictatorship and, although he engages tentatively in a critical if brief analysis of its effects, he ignores for instance how Hitler's wars, especially those carried out in the East, were conducted as total wars, in the name of a total ideology that aimed at total domination.

For Schmitt, dissociating himself from Hitler meant associating his fate as one of those defeated to the fate of Europe.[26] Both Schmitt and Europe had lost; thus they ran the risk of having to surrender their legacy and reputation. Here Schmitt somehow imagined his position as being at odds with the emerging postcolonial configuration of the old continent, with its relativization and decentering.[27] This allowed him to reinvent himself as the last representative of a vanishing Europe in a new technical age ruled by two non-European universalist powers: the United States and the Soviet Union.[28] But, if the future was lost to the Europeans, and even if being right meant being in the dark, what was the meaning of writing on his personal experiences? Such writing was meaningful to him, because he transmuted and elevated them into political knowledge with a critical twist, as he sought to come to terms with the postwar situation in a volatile moment of change, during exceptional times. By inventing an intellectual place for illiberalism, Schmitt sought to reaffirm his own trajectory together with that of Europe. It is interesting to note that, during the same period, Karl Jaspers, perhaps one of the most renowned philosophers and public intellectuals at the time and a witness to the catastrophe, publicly asked about the collective guilt of Germans and their political and historical responsibility. He will later go on to claim that a critique of the Nazi past was needed for a new democracy.[29] Schmitt took the opposite direction. In this sense, the prison writings anticipated more recent populist attempts to absolve the Germans of any guilt for the crimes committed by the Nazis and can be seen as a foundational text for those who desire a new antiliberalism, postfascist and authoritarian.

Besides an attempt at self-vindication and notwithstanding its unapologetic stance, Schmitt blended prophecy and realism in order to diagnose and denounce the ills that plagued the old continent in the post-Eurocentric global age of the emerging Cold War. This was a new world, which grew from the ruins of the international interstate order and lacked balance and orientation, governed and decided upon by Schmitt's two political enemies: liberalism and communism, the West and the East. He thought he was witnessing a poststatist age of global disorder and spatial chaos, of conflict and anomy—an "intermediary" stage in world history situated between the old international interstate order and a coming new *nomos* of the earth. In other words, this was a transitional stage without territorial distinctions and spatial divisions. Lacking free colonial soil while the universalization of the principle of sovereign statehood was underway, the globe was left defenseless against civil wars, absolute enemies, and motorized partisans.[30] Schmitt described else-where this postcolonial transitional period situated in an indistinct zone between peace and war—the one he experienced from his cell—as the age of global civil wars, the "epoch of total war, of wars of extermination, and of the partisans."[31]

For Schmitt, his time in prison, the time of this text, were times of civil war on a global scale. The prison writings reflect and respond to this abnormal and extreme situation and provide the broader political and historical context of Schmitt's postwar political and legal theory. They also give a preliminary but solid account of the theoretical development of Schmitt's key concepts, such as "civil war" and "the enemy." An exception once again animates his work. And, if there is a common theme that runs through this short text, this is the theme of civil war as an exception that is becoming a norm. Hence, like his "brothers" Jean Bodin and Thomas Hobbes—both thinkers of the state and both "entirely formed by civil wars"—Schmitt saw himself as writing about politics and law during civil wars.[32] In a way, all three formulated their political ideas with and against the question of civil war. But, unlike the French and the English, the German introduced a global dimension in his later explorations and abandoned the state as the central organizational principle of political and legal reasoning. His civil wars are global and define the concrete political reality, the spirit of his historical times, and Schmitt's own fate.

* * *

This book appeared the same year as *The Nomos of the Earth*, *The Plight of European Jurisprudence*, and *A Pan-European Interpretation of Donoso Cortés*.[33] All are important works in their own right, written in the first half of the 1940s—with the exception of the prison writings; all seem to signal a belated intellectual and public comeback and to announce Schmitt's definitive return to postwar Germany. This publishing event resulted in an intellectually active and vibrant decade that eventually culminated in *Theory of the Partisan* in 1963 and *Political Theology II* in 1970—his last two major books. The prison writings thus announce this new and last period in Schmitt's controversial life and remain a key text for understanding his widely influential thinking and for pondering over its overall significance and present relevance. But, if this book starts with a personal call—a demand for radical self-interrogation—it turns quickly into an unapologetic albeit erudite self-justification that reasserts its unity of meaning and purpose by deploying a suspicious dialectical resolution between loss and recuperation, suffering and redemption. The prison writings conclude with Schmitt's auspicious vision of "the rich fruit from which meaning springs by right" and the expectant realization that he is not after all "naked but rather clothed and on the way to a house."[34] Clothed and free, indeed, the text ends with the hopeful anticipation of his release from detention on May 13, 1947.[35]

January 2017

1

Conversation with Eduard Spranger

Who are you? *Tu quis es?* This is an unfathomable question. I plunged deeply into it at the end of June 1945 as Eduard Spranger, the famous philosopher and teacher, awaited my response to a questionnaire. On this occasion he told me that my lectures were extremely spirited but that I myself—my personality and my essence—remained opaque. That was a serious accusation, which meant: what you think and say may be interesting and clear; but what you are, your self, your essence, is murky and unclear.

I was shocked by this. What use are the most beautiful lectures, what help the clearest concepts, what use is the mind? It is a matter of essence. Or of being and existence. In short, a difficult problem, not yet solved by philosophy, descended upon my soul. Is transparency of thinking even compatible with opacity of essence? And how are such contradictions possible? Age-old and highly modern contradictions stung me and sank in: thought and being, knowledge and life, intellect against instinct, mind against soul, whole sequences of such antitheses ran wildly through my mind.

What should I now do? Should I strive to become transparent? Or should I try to deliver the proof that I am in reality not so opaque but rather—at least for benevolent radiographers [*Durchleuchter*]—fully transparent?

I looked at my interrogator and thought: Who are *you*, in fact, to question me? Whence your superiority? What is the essence of power that empowers and emboldens you to pose such questions to me—questions that are intended to challenge me and thus are, in their final effect, only snares and traps?

Such counterquestions were obvious. But it does not suit me to pose counterquestions. My essence may by opaque, but in any case it is defensive. I am a contemplative person and may tend to sharp formulations, but not in order to take the offensive or the counteroffensive. My essence is slow, soundless, and pliable, like that of a calm river—like the Mosel: *tacito rumore Mosellae* ["under Mosella's quiet rustle"].

But I am weak on the defensive as well. I have too little practical interest in myself and too much theoretical interest in the ideas of my opponent, even when they appear as prosecutors. I am too curious about the intellectual presuppositions of each accusation, each charge, and each accuser. For this reason I am neither a good defendant nor a good prosecutor. Nevertheless, I still prefer to be a defendant rather than a prosecutor. The *j'accuse* types may play their role on the world stage. To me, the prosecutorial is even more sinister than the inquisitorial. Perhaps in my case this can be traced back to theological roots. For *Diabolus* means "the prosecutor."[1]

I am lost if my opponent is very vicious and I am not very good. But this was not the case here. My questioner meant to be strict but not vicious. I, on the other hand, did not mean anything. I wanted and expected nothing from him.

I was happy to see him again, for my old love for him had not yet been extinguished. For this reason I could see him, while he did not see me. He was completely imbued with the sense of being right and of having been proven right. He was therefore filled with the sense of being right in every regard: ethically, philosophically, pedagogically, historically, and politically. All that was right, all that rightness could provide, *iusta causa* and *res iudicata*, was on his side.

I know as a jurist what that means. I know the *small* tragedy of human righteousness [*Rechthabens*]. I also know European international law and its history. I am today—Quincy Wright notwithstanding—the only teacher of law on this earth who has recorded and experienced the problem of just war, including unfortunately civil war, in all of its depth and causes. Thus I also know the *great* tragedy of human dogmatism.

Therefore I am defenseless. Defenseless but in no sense destroyed. Many years ago I had shown this man— this philosopher and teacher across from whom I now sat as a person he had called into question—all the honor and devotion of my soul. In memory of this time and in the knowledge that I have never done or wished anything evil upon him, I answered him as you answer a philosopher, not a questionnaire. I said to him: my essence may well not be fully transparent, but my case can be named with the help of a name discovered by a great poet. It is the poor, unworthy, and yet nevertheless authentic case of a Christian Epimetheus.

From this answer, however, no further conversation ensued.

Summer 1945

2

Remarks in Response to a Radio Speech by Karl Mannheim

In 1945 Karl Mannheim, the sociologist, developed the program for a new European university on London radio. For him as for any serious thinker, it goes without saying that without scholarly freedom there can be no university, or at least no institution worthy of this great name in the sense it has within the European tradition and western rationalism. Yet what constitutes this scholarly freedom and what is its fundamental precondition?

Karl Mannheim provides the answer: the precondition of scholarly freedom is "a fundamental curiosity that wishes to understand every other group and every other person in their otherness." We can build on this answer both in a philosophical–epistemological [*erkenntniskritischer*] and in a historical–sociological fashion. We may interpret it as the presupposition of a factual–scholarly interest that avoids the dead ends in which the fronts and counterfronts of world civil war, both the open and the latent one, meet their spiritual death. Avoiding this would be the main issue in the present European situation. For in some respects the kind of civil war carried out in the confessional wars of the sixteenth and seventeenth centuries in Europe and on colonial soil is repeating itself.

Without the presupposition of a "fundamental curiosity" in the sense of a restless drive to continue questioning there can really be no intellectual freedom, at least no freedom of scholarship. Now, can that which the German mind produced in the way of scholarly achievements in the 12 years from 1933 to 1945 be an occasion for such curiosity? Or is the interest that German researchers and scholars, but also German poets, painters, and musicians deserve over these 12 years to be attended to solely on the basis of the announcements and proclamations that were broadcast over the amplifiers of that era's public sphere?

It is well known that, in a totalitarian one-party system, everything that is not forbidden is compulsory. If a hundred-percent totality [*Totalität*] in fact existed and if the only thing to be considered valid were what the loudspeakers of the system barked out into the world, then the issue would already be settled. If what stands in the spotlight of a constantly recorded and licensed public sphere were the only thing worthy of notice, and if, in addition, merely entering this public sphere were construed as unconditional spiritual submission, then the scholarly work of these twelve years would indeed merit no special recognition. Then the sociological and mass-psychological techniques of the apparatus would at best be worthy of some interest, namely in the context of the sociological problem of the control of the masses through the use of science—a problem that is acute not only in Germany.

For scholarship itself, however, one cannot content oneself with the façade of an artificially organized public sphere. In reality, specifically new questions emerge in confrontation with a situation that arises within a system of sharpened controls: above all, the question of the degree of totality, pretended or real, and the further question of whether the sphere under consideration here can be ascertained. One would have to ask to what extent it is even possible for a political ruler to achieve such a grip on the intellectual productivity of an entire people that no free thought and no reservations in fact remain. The possibility of a complete, hundred-percent totality is a sociological problem of the first order.

It may have come to pass, now and then in world history, that entire civilizations were eradicated. European intellectual history does not know many such cases. The spirit of western rationalism has until now, even in dire cases of political terror, awakened mental and intellectual forces that did not come to the surface; at least initially it did not wish to do so. The mind has its pride, its tactics, its ineluctable freedom, and, if you excuse the expression, even its guardian angel, and it has all this not merely in emigration but also inwardly, even in the claws of the Leviathan itself. In Europe, the mind has known until now how to find its crypts and catacombs, its new methods and forms. *Tyrannum licet decipere* ["one is allowed to deceive a tyrant"]. This sentence stands prominently at the beginning of the entire doctrine of tyranny in the Middle Ages, which at the same time was a doctrine of *potestas spiritualis* [spiritual power] and without this concrete precondition is nothing but an abominable doctrine of civil war.

Now, however, modern natural science places monstrous instruments of power at the disposal of rulers and the legal, quasi-legal, and illegal possibilities of a modern system are not to be compared with the opportunities available to a medieval power. This trend will continue in the future. In Germany, the mind has once again outmaneuvered [*über-spielt*] the Leviathan. I conclude from this that the humanities will outmaneuver the natural sciences and will force them to transform themselves into humanities. From technically enhanced coercion and technically enhanced control there emerge new forms of novel thinking and speaking that evade this coercion and control. This is true in general, with regard to every kind of terror and discrimination. It is true not only for Germany and not only for the 12 years [of Nazi rule].

Germany has long been a relatively small, intellectually non-circumscribed and non-circumscribable space in the middle of Europe, a junction and a transit country for forces and ideas from the North and the South, the West and the East. Germany has never decided in a clear and unified way [between these competing geographical influences], and was unable to do so because it could not submit itself to any of the questions that descended upon it from abroad. Here lies the secret of its weakness and its superiority. As a result of the still unresolved struggle between Catholicism and Protestantism, the German mind has remained open, and in this state of suspension it has developed a great tradition of the most thorough research and the boldest criticism. In the nineteenth century Hegelianism joined in. It became historically effective in Marxism. In this way [German] openness underwent an extraordinary expansion. Of course, the educated class grew weaker from generation to generation after 1848 and was in the end almost demoralized. Nevertheless, it was in no sense dehumanized and destroyed, even in the 12 years from 1933 to 1945. It was full of fear in the face of any civil war and showed little aptitude for conspiracies and plots. Thus it could become the prey of a sworn society: an easy, but in the end merely perfunctory prey. Only he who knows his prey better than it knows itself can conquer.

The ineradicable individualism of the German [character] retained its force in the face of this perfunctory conquest as well. Its astounding susceptibility to being organized is only the foreground of its astounding ego armor [*Ich-Verpanzerung*]. The silent, tried-and-tested tradition of withdrawal to a private interiority subsisted, along with a great readiness for conscientious cooperation with whatever the current legal government mandated. And positivists as well as pietists could easily come to the same practical conclusion, namely that a government unopposed by even the shadow of a countergovernment was legal. Nowhere else has the separation between interior and exterior been driven to this complete disjunction between inside and outside. The inner, complete Gleichschaltung of this kind of educated class is every bit as difficult as its external Gleichschaltung is smooth and easy.

On the other hand, the mental basis of the Gleichschaltung, its so-called Weltanschauung, was in itself much too intellectually confused to yield a consistent doctrine and, with it, the norm for a total registration. The way the party program was worded allowed for many conflicting interpretations, which gained currency in different instances and in different years, in the most diverse ways. Numerous directions, streams and movements, groups, circles, and alliances emerged in Germany since 1900—since the beginning of domestic protest against the official Germany of the time. They all contributed in some way to the success of the great mass movement that fell into Hitler's hands. They were also all somehow appropriated. But they were either too deep or too dull, too manifold or too idiosyncratic, to be capable of becoming a more or less coherent intellectual formation. The existing Christian churches and Marxist doctrine were scarcely impacted in their intellectual content by the montage of slogans from the party. The sociological and intellectual-historical explanation of this kind of party is a problem in its own right. In any case it is improbable that such an ideological bovigus[1] could have consumed the education and intelligence of the entire German people in the course of 12 years and that all intellectual productivity would have been absorbed by this combination of non-committal ambiguity and the most servile clarity.

The external terror became more spasmodic in the process, but the chances of a mental totality grew ever weaker. Every amplifier brings a falsification of meaning, even for those who consider themselves masters of the amplifier. Danger awakens new forces among those who have not succumbed [to the official ideology]. The mind and intelligence put forward multiple forms of politeness, correctness, and irony, and ultimately their silence, against the clamor of public activity. A judgment regarding achievements in such a situation can thus not simply be passed from the outside. The person judging must remain aware of a few basic sociological truths, above all things regarding the eternal link between protection and obedience.

A researcher and scholar cannot select the political regime according to his wishes either. In general he accepts it initially as a loyal citizen, like every other person. If the situation then becomes completely anomalous and nobody from the outside protects him from the terror within, he must determine the boundaries of his loyalty himself, namely when the situation becomes so abnormal that one no longer knows where even his closest friend really stands. The duty to unleash a civil war, to conduct sabotage, and to become a martyr has its limits. Here one should grant something to the victims of such situations and should not be allowed to judge only from the outside. Plato was an aide to the tyrants of Syracuse and taught that one should not be permitted to refuse good advice even to the enemy. Thomas More, the patron saint of intellectual freedom, went through many phases and made astounding concessions to the tyrant before things reached the point where he became a martyr and saint. In any case the old sentence of Macrobius' *Saturnalia*—*non possum scribere in eum qui potest proscribere* ["it is not possible to write against one who has the power to proscribe"]—is valid in all times of political concentration of power and for every publicist.

In the summer of 1938 in Germany, a book was published that included the following passage: "If in a [particular] country only the public sphere organized by the state still has any validity, then the soul of a people embarks on the secret path leading inward; then the counterforce of silence and of quiet grows." Benito Cereno, the hero of Herman Melville's novella,[2] was elevated to a symbol of the position of the intelligentsia in a mass system. In September 1939 *Die Marmorklippen* [*On the Marble Cliffs*][3] appeared, a book that portrays with great daring the abysses concealed behind the orderly masks of nihilism. Despite fanatical controls, many works of authentic art emerged even in the genre of painting, then discriminated against; and they found genuine protection and true support. In all areas of the natural sciences and humanities one will discover great achievements, so much so that intellectual curiosity does not suddenly fail. The mind is in essence free and brings its own freedom with it. It will have to prove its freedom in the dangerous situations of modern mass organization as well. But the measure of its success cannot be sought too far afield from its context.

Corresponding to this intellectual freedom is the inalienable right to a scholarly hearing. Our scholarly work has nothing to fear from the forum of the mind, nothing to conceal and nothing to regret. The discussion of its mistakes will be very informative. We look forward to the fundamental curiosity mentioned above and to a free public sphere. But we cannot do without the gains of a difficult time of trial and will not forget what we experienced in the danger of those twelve years: the difference between a genuine and a false public sphere, and the counteracting force of silence and quiet.

* * *

I want to try to reach Karl Mannheim with these answering remarks.[4] "Understanding"[5] has been discussed so often and so much among sociologists that it would be good to test this understanding, for once, in a desperate situation, and not only in the atmosphere of well-organized sociologists' conferences. I am reminded of some good conversations with Karl Mannheim. Perhaps he understands that scholarly curiosity plagues me at all times and today no less than it does him, and that the loudspeakers of today have just as little authority for me as the loudspeakers of yesterday. Above all, he will not misunderstand my reference to his formula of scholarly curiosity as an appeal to the victor. His formulation contains too much of the dialectic of the objective mind for that. He speaks of the comprehension of the other in its otherness. Whoever makes use of such phrases knows that the way of the mind also leads through errors, in which the mind remains the mind, even in its error. Thus it is written in a classic passage with a famous sentence. This sentence of the master[6] is no charter, least of all for perfidy, but rather a letter of safe conduct whose handwriting the sons of freedom can read.

Winter 1945/6

3

Historiographia in nuce

Alexis de Tocqueville

1

A saying that I heard often in my youth still rings in my ears today: *History is written by the victor*. This sounds like an order and surely originated with a soldier.

The first historical book I read as a boy was Annegarn's *Weltgeschichte* [*World History*],[1] a good household book representing German history from a Catholic standpoint. The Catholics of the time, around 1900, were in any case not the victors in a Germany governed by Prussia, and their historiographers stood on the defensive. I was not aware of any of this as a youth. A boy who enthusiastically reads history books does not give a thought to who actually writes these beautiful stories. I was enraptured by the valiant Annegarn and did not dwell on problems of historiography.

Then gradually I got to know the victors of my time and their historiographers. Thus the sociological meaning of that saying about victorious historiographers became clear to me. The saying now meant that the national–liberal historians of the Bismarck Empire, Sybel, Treitschke, and their successors, were the great writers of history. In comparison, the defeated Austrians or the French were not worthy of notice, to say nothing of the Danes, the Poles, and the Italians [*Ultramontanen*].[2] Nevertheless, as World War I approached, one could sometimes also hear a warning, namely that we must stick together in order not to find ourselves in the role of the vanquished. Otherwise to all the other misfortunes of a lost war would be added the triumph of the victors' historians over our historians.

In all such sayings about war, one thought only of the European land war of the nineteenth century—a military war organized by states. One did not think of civil war. There are many significant proverbs about war in general. Poets and philosophers, historians and soldiers have spoken of war. Unfortunately, everything that has been said about war receives its ultimate and bitter meaning in civil war. Many quote the sentence of Heraclitus: "War is the father of all things."[3] But few dare to think of civil war in this context.

2

For a long time now I have held Alexis de Tocqueville to have been the greatest historian of the nineteenth century. He seems somewhat old-fashioned and courtly, but for all that he is one of those rare historians who did not succumb to the histrionic tendencies of their century. It is wonderful how his gaze pierces the foregrounds of revolutions and restorations to perceive the fateful core of the development that takes place behind contradictory fronts and slogans—a development used by all parties, from right to left, for driving things on to ever further centralization and democratization.

If I say that the gaze of this historian pierces, this should not be taken to mean that he has a strained and tensely penetrating gaze. He does not have the zeal of a sociological or psychological debunker or the vanity of a skeptic, but he harbors no metaphysical ambitions either. He does not wish to find eternal laws of the world-historical process: neither three-stage laws nor cultural cycles. He speaks not of things in which he is not existentially involved, of Indians and Egyptians, of Etruscans and Hittites. He does not seat himself, as do the great Hegel and the wise Ranke, next to God in the royal box of the world theater. He is a moralist in the sense established by the French tradition, like Montesquieu, and at the same time a painter in the sense of the French concept of *peinture*. His gaze is gentle and clear and always somewhat sad. He possesses intellectual courage, but out of politeness and loyalty he gives everyone a chance and makes no loud displays of despair. Thus in 1849 he became for a few months the foreign minister of President Louis Napoleon, whom he clearly perceived as a histrionic figure. The chapter he devotes to this experience in his memoirs is very topical. In general one recognizes him best in his *Souvenirs* [*Recollections*].[4] No historian has anything comparable to Tocqueville to offer, with this wonderful book. But what elevates him far above all other historians of the nineteenth century is the great prognosis that stands at the end of the first volume of *Democracy in America*.[5]

Tocqueville's prognosis states that humankind will irresistibly and inevitably continue further along the path it has long been on, toward centralization and democratization. But the forward-looking historian does not rest content with having determined a general developmental tendency. He identifies simply and clearly the concrete historical powers that [will] carry and accomplish this development: America and Russia. As different and opposed as they might be,

they both nevertheless come, along very different paths—
the one through free, the other through dictatorial forms
of organization—to the same result of a centralized and
democratized humankind.

3

It is in fact extraordinary that a young European jurist could
have conceived of such a prognosis over a hundred years ago,
when the dominant picture of the world of his age was still
entirely Eurocentric. Hegel had died a few years earlier, in
1831, without having identified the two new world powers
as bearers of a new development. The most astonishing fact is
that the French historian names the new powers of America
and Russia together in this concrete way, although neither
of them was yet industrialized. Two emerging giants, both
formed by the European spirit but still not European, will
confront each other directly, beyond the borders of little
Europe and without consulting it.

What Tocqueville predicted in this way was no vague
oracle, no prophetic vision, and no general historical–
philosophical construction. It was a real prognosis, won on
the basis of objective observations and superior diagnoses,
registered with the courage of a European intelligence and
expressed with all the precision of a French mind. With this
prognosis the European self-consciousness changed, and
there began a new phase of historical self-contextualization.
The wider strata of society became conscious of this shift
only later, through the spotlight of open emergency and the
amplifiers of the German headline "Demise of the West."
The problem is not one of today, and not one of yesterday.
The first modern contribution to this secular theme comes

from Tocqueville. Up to the present day this remains also the most significant contribution, because it is the most concrete. Deep historical truths find their clearest expression at the moment of their ascent.

4

Tocqueville was one of the vanquished. All forms of defeat converged in him, and not accidentally and only unluckily, but rather fatefully and existentially. As an aristocrat, he was on the losing side in the civil war, the worst kind of war, which also brings with it the worst kind of defeat. He belonged to the social class that was defeated by the French Revolution. As a liberal, he foresaw the no longer liberal Revolution of 1848 and was fatally affected by the outbreak of its horrors. As a Frenchman, he belonged to the nation that was defeated by England, Russia, Austria, and Prussia after a 20-year coalition war. Thus he was on the losing side in an international world war. As a European, he found himself in the role of the defeated, for he foresaw the development that, over Europe's head, made two new powers, America and Russia, into the bearers and inheritors of an irresistible centralization and democratization. Finally, as a Christian—which he remained in accordance with the beliefs of his fathers, through baptism and tradition—he succumbed to the scientific agnosticism of the age.

Nevertheless he did not become what he, more than any other, seemed predestined to be: a Christian Epimetheus. He lacked the footing in salvific history that would preserve his historical idea of Europe against despair. Europe was lost without the idea of a *katechon*.[6] Tocqueville knew no *katechon*. Instead he sought intelligent compromises. He himself felt the weakness of these compromises just as did his opponents, who for that reason mocked him.

Thus he became one of the vanquished who accepted his defeat. *C'est un vaincu qui accepte sa défaite* ["only someone defeated accepts his defeat"]. Guizot said this of him, and Sainte-Beuve spread it eagerly around. It was ill meant. The literary critic uses it as a poisoned arrow in order to fatally strike the famous historian. But God alters the meaning of such spiteful remarks and makes them into the testimony of an unwanted and unexpected depth of insight. In this way the viciously intended phrase can even serve to help us divine the secret [*arcanum*] of the greatness that elevates the defeated Frenchman above all other historiographers of his century.

5

In the autumn of 1940, as France lay defeated on the ground, I had a discussion with a Yugoslavian, the Serbian poet Ivo Andrić, whom I love very much. We had met in a shared connoisseurship and in the veneration of Léon Bloy. The Serb told me the following story from the mythology of his people: Marko Kraljević, the hero of the Serbian saga, fought for an entire day with a powerful Turk and laid him out after a hard struggle. As he killed the defeated enemy, a serpent that had been sleeping upon the heart of the dead man awoke and spoke to Marko: You were lucky that I slept through your battle. Then the hero cried out: Woe is me! I killed a man who was stronger than me!

I retold this story to some friends and acquaintances at the time and also to Ernst Jünger, who was stationed as an officer of the army of occupation in Paris. We were all deeply impressed. But it was clear to us that the victors of today do not allow themselves to be impressed by such medieval stories. This, too, belongs to your great prognosis, poor, defeated Tocqueville!

Summer 1946

4

Two Graves

For 40 years a strong current has repeatedly carried me out of the west of Germany toward Berlin and held me there until the present day, against all my tendencies and instincts, against all plans and resolutions. I have had my residence in Berlin for 18 years, without really wanting to but nevertheless without being able to get away. It has been the same for many Germans of my age and social class. A giant turbine has drawn us in here. A maelstrom has dropped us to this place. Berlin has become our fate, and we, its victims, have become Berlin's fate. For us, this problematic, volatile [*auf-brecherische*] capital city was more of a passage than a real city or a domicile. For numerous residents it was nothing but a restless workplace with good theaters and a lot of night business, made bearable through many trips to the lake or into the mountains, a termite colony obsessed with innovation, a Promethean furnace, and finally a crematorium. Was it also overall, viewed historically, nothing more than a crematorium and, in the end, not even that any longer but rather just a garbage can and a pile of debris?

It was much more and something completely different. There are in Berlin not only debris and rubble but also graves.

A city attains its historical standing through its graves. It may be that churches and palaces dominate the picture, but the deeper effect emanates from its graves. They broadcast their songs of the dead inaudibly and ineffably. Rome is a holy city because of its graves, only secondarily because of its churches and palaces. Berlin has nothing of the holy city about it. We do not wish to speak of its churches here. But there are substantial [*wirkliche*] graves in Berlin. Not only simple, decent, honest graves that have not been destroyed by any handicraft experiments; not only graves of the poor, the foreign, and the unknown, which move one more deeply than false mausoleums; but also graves that ground a historical dignity.

I think here not of the famous philosophers Fichte and Hegel. Their graves did not become famous. Such idealistic thinkers have too questionable a relationship to the resurrection of the flesh for their own graves to be able to hold the seeds of historical expectations. Fichte's immortal *I* will somehow domesticate for itself [*sich ... anbändigen*] a new *Not-I*, and Hegel's absolute spirit will settle somewhere in freedom in a new residence. There are some dignified graves of artists and scholars in Berlin. The Humboldt grave in Tegel is the perfect document of a successful classicism. There are also helpless graves that are the final expression of a helpless existence, such as the grave of Bruno Bauer in the cemetery of the former Rixdorf—a stone with the false title "Dr. Bruno Bauer," about which the old licentiate in theology would have smiled knowingly.

But what do such graves set up, and what perishes with them when they are destroyed or relocated? At the Invalidenfriedhof [Invalids' Cemetery] there are real graves of soldiers, especially of those granted the order Pour le

Mérite. As far as I am aware, in the old days Ernst Jünger had reserved the right to take his place among them. I no longer know whether he continues today to hold on to this claim. It is difficult to speak of such things, for we who are still living on earth know no more about our real grave than we do of life after death. The grave still belongs to the overall picture of our earthly appearance. We learn as boys and experience as old men the cry of Solon: *Nemo ante mortem beatus* ["No one can be called happy before he dies"]. We can add, *ante sepulcrum* ["before the tomb"], and we can say, *beatus vel miser* ["happy or wretched"]. Of these things we can certainly speak. We are even obligated to become aware of a current problem of a new kind. The modern procedures appropriate to the age of progress have also perfected the methods of disposing of the corpses of political enemies and have modernized the ancient theme of Antigone.

I know of two graves in Berlin that bear witness to something and that make this destroyed city be, for me, more than the ashes of a Promethean furnace. Two German poets have found their graves here, and in such a way that both of these graves say more about our true [history], that is, our history of suffering, than the graves in the Fürstengruft [ducal burial chapel] at Weimar: the grave of Kleist at Wannsee and the grave of Theodor Däubler at the cemetery on the Heerstraße. On the basis of these graves alone, Berlin is no mere crematorium and no pile of debris.

* * *

Heinrich von Kleist carried in his being the dichotomy between the West and the East. As a young man he considered becoming a soldier under Napoleon; later on enmity against the foreign conqueror took hold of his soul. Napoleon—that was the West. Kleist could have had patience and waited. To date, the East has demonstrated more patience than the West. Slavic patience will become the master of our guilt.[1] Of course in Berlin there was too much intellectual ferment [*Geist*] for a great deal of patience to have been possible. But also, intellectually speaking, Napoleon could not have conquered Prussia permanently. Only he who knows his prey better than it knows itself can conquer, and there is no question that the Prussian philosophers of that time knew more about the ideas of the West than the West of that time even suspected about the powers of the East.

Kleist's hatred of the French was not yet an option for the East, which back then did not even exist in today's sense. But in the concrete world-political situation, hatred of the French was already an option for Russia—the land power that had brought Napoleon low, with all the consequences that emerged from this in the course of the nineteenth century—and both for Prussia, with a Germany governed from Prussia, and for a Europe overshadowed by a powerful Germany. It was in any case an updating of the strong eastern elements within Prussia's own mode of being. One year before his death, Kleist wrote the inexhaustible, always astounding essay "On the Marionette Theater" [*Über das Marionettentheater*].[2] At the end a bear appears who, with unerring instinct, proves superior to all, even to those with the most intelligent technique. He exhausts the best foil fencer simply because he does not react to feints. This bearer of unknown powers is a mythical symbol and already stands in the lineage of a deep opposition between East and West.

The opposition runs right across the middle of Germany, halfway through Germany's heart. Among the classics of German literature it is still completely unthinkable in this form. Nevertheless, it appears from the East already in the eighteenth century. A remarkable document from this period is the appeal directed to Frederick the Great from Königsberg, in the year 1776, by the quintessential philosopher of the German East, Johann Georg Hamann. The greater philosopher Hamann appealed to the King of Prussia against the philosopher of Sanssouci. The philosopher of Sanssouci, that was the West; the King of Prussia, the East. But who, in the age of Voltaire, should have read such a letter and understood such an appeal? By contrast, in the century to follow, a left-wing Hegelian like Bruno Bauer could opt for the East in full world-historical consciousness.

In the autumn of 1935 I was in Wannsee, at Kleist's grave, with the poet Konrad Weiß and two Westphalian friends. Konrad Weiß published a magnificent essay about this. In Weiß's historical imaginary [*Geschichtsbild*], which is entirely Marian, Kleist's female forms were wonderfully Christian, while the women of Goethe were either idealistically pallid or adorably romantic. We did not speak about the death of Kleist. In October of 1944 I visited the grave together with my daughter Anima. The old, modest gravestone, which had a certain tradition, had been removed and replaced by a modern, simple stone. The old aphoristic inscription had had to give way to a verse from *The Prince of Homburg*: "Now, o immortality, you are entirely mine!"[3]— which sounded all too ambitious in this place. The carrion birds of the approaching epidemic of suicides already buzzed in the air. It was a dreadful hour. But I did not want to talk about this with a child of 13. In the meantime, my own experiences have driven me to think further and to say what has become clear to me.

Kleist's grave is the grave of a suicide. He killed himself deliberately and advisedly; he died by his own hand. No idealistic rhetoric can embellish or dissemble this fact. On the old gravestone stood the verse:

Here he sought death
and found immortality.

Was it really death that he sought? The death wish [*Todeslust*] is not death. And would anyone [claim to] know what he really found? I think today in horror about the fact that this suicide, carried out in November 1811, could already have been a harbinger of those suicides that were committed in early 1945 in exactly this part of Berlin and in a particular social class.

From a modern poet, indeed the most modern of all, from Theodor Däubler, comes the line: "The plants teach us the soft dying of the heath/en."[4]

I do not believe in this soft dying of the heath/en or in its plantlike character. Where the heathens were well ahead of us [*Was die Heiden ... vor uns voraushatten*] in this regard, and what a European of the twentieth century attempts in vain to reproduce, is something else, namely the power to make a sacrament out of a suicide. Only a single person has brought this off in a way understandable to us: the Stoic philosopher [Seneca], who solemnly took the step into the realm of freedom and in doing so saw the last—in fact the only—possibility of proving his human dignity and of preserving his moral freedom. In my life I have known two men who have taken their own lives, perhaps in part with such motivations: Otto Baensch, a neo-Kantian philosopher, who died in despair in 1936, and Wilhelm Ahlmann, who by dying put himself and his friends beyond the reach of further police interrogation in December of 1944.

Only in times of civil war does the exemplary significance of this form of death come into its own. A famous historical case is the demise of the philosopher Condorcet, who took poison during the Terror of 1793 and thus evaded the Terror and by the same move succumbed to it. Yet this is already modern. In truth Seneca remains the only priest of this highly philosophical sacrament. He was a contemporary both of the heathen Emperor Nero and of the Christian apostle Paul. His speech already possessed something of the growth of the word become flesh. Upon his act there already rests a radiance of sanctification that only the death of the living God on the cross could have granted. Seneca's nephew Lucan must also be mentioned here, for he is the poet of civil war. Both were contemporaries of the unique, unrepeatable, constantly present events that founded and [still] maintain our eon. For us the shimmering light of the Stoic suicide comes from there, from the origin of our eon. It is only a lunar light, like that of all humanistic attempts at religion, and is not capable of producing sacramental forms.

Kleist was no Stoic. His suicide was no act of combat in a civil war either. The desire for death had gripped him. He knew the fear and sought the voluptuousness of the grave. He sought the bed of the empress. Yet he did not become a Euphorion[5] of the desire for death. He was no heathen—neither an unbroken, pre-Christian heathen nor a voluntary heathen in the sense associated with the modern lust for life and desperate secularity. He was driven far beyond the elements of death and the grave. He wanted to open the gates of an afterworld, to force them, and did not want to be alone in this. He took a companion with him, a victim who offered

herself to him. As he went to his death with solemn pro-
nouncements of his serenity, with a woman as companion,
victim, and witness, he sought a passage into another realm
and attempted the rite of opening of this passage. His act
exaggerated the element and sought to attain a sacrament.

And yet he found no sacrament prepared for him. He did
not even find the sign of the cross in the name of the Holy
Trinity, a sign whose salvific power Annette von Droste-
Hülshoff had experienced and to which she bore witness
in one of her strongest poems.[6] Kleist's leap into the realm
of freedom became in this way an act of violence; and the
companion, instead of a witness, was in the end merely the
helpless echo of male despair. It was the act of violence of
a German poet whom the humanism of the German classics and the idealism of German philosophy had left unre-
deemed, because neither could offer him a sacrament—or
even a sign. Both humanism and idealism are, as Konrad
Weiß says, luminous [*lichtvoll*] but vacuous. In contrast, a
luster from Maria Immaculata fell upon the female figures
of Kleist, upon his Amazons as much as upon his sleepwalk-
ing girls; and Maria, the helpful mother, cannot have left the
poet of such female figures without her assistance. A hint of
her heavenly beneficence breaks up [*löst*] the stiff lament of
this grave.

* * *

The other grave lies in the ranks of an individualistically
tended metropolitan cemetery at the Reichssportfeld
[Imperial Sports Complex]. It is the grave of the poet
whose line on "the soft dying of the heath/en" I just quoted.
Theodor Däubler came to Berlin from the South, from
Trieste, via Rome, Florence, and Paris. When he arrived

here in 1912, the shadows of the approaching world war
already lay upon Wilhelmine Germany and its capital. The
inquisitive intellectualism of this Berlin was still able, in the
field of music, to follow Richard Strauß well. In painting it
reacted in a lively fashion to the problematic of new concepts
of space. In language and literature it was too self-satisfied
to have been capable of sensitivity [*hellhörig*]. Young birds of
death, like Georg Heym and Georg Trakl, did not remain
unnoticed. Nothing remained unnoticed; and certainly not
Däubler. But what should one do with this poor, unkempt
Bohemian? He was a colossus of a man and had a colossal
stack of works with him, the thick, three-volume epic of *The
Northern Lights*.[7] Johannes Schlaf, with his nose for cosmic
scents [*mit seinen kosmischen Witterungen*], flagged it immediately as the epic of Europe. But who else could believe,
in 1912, that this was the great European poet who had
taken upon himself the intellectual and artistic completion
of French and Italian art, he, endlessly more modern than all
the aesthetes and literati whose pride it was to be modern?

The unkempt colossus was in reality a genius of European
sensibility, a genius in languages, such as only an Illyrian can
be. To that degree he was the modern, artistic counterim-
age to his theological fourth-century compatriot, Jerome,
father of the Latin Vulgate whose phonetic beauty we have
heard and felt since Charles Péguy. What the European
impressionism of the nineteenth century, what futurism,
cubism, and expressionism had broken open from many
chaotic starting points found its unexpected fulfillment in
the German language. The German poem became a new
wonderwork of sound, color, and thought. It became a score
whose tonal and coloristic plenitude is continuously intoned,
interpreted, and conducted by the reader and hearer. Many

poets were involved in the linguistic transformation, among them great names such as Stefan George and Rainer Maria Rilke. But it was first through Däubler that the German language became the pure wonder instrument of a new tonality.

Däubler was often in Berlin, though he had neither domicile nor home [*Heimat*] there. He loved this passage into the unforeseeable, despite its destabilizing [*aufbrecherischen*] obsession with innovation and despite ugly experiences with its people. He penned no hymn to Berlin, but rather an ode to Rome, a song to Milan, hymns to Italian cities, and magnificent beginnings of a hymn to the Köln Cathedral and other German places. But he wanted to be buried in Berlin after he had traveled the long path from the Mediterranean through Western Europe.

"The wanderer would lie down with the waiting."[8]

Rilke and Stefan George made their way to Switzerland and found their graves there. Däubler, the poet of gnostically illuminated verses about the resurrection of the flesh, laid himself down with the waiting in Berlin, in the sand of the March of Brandenburg. On his headstone stands the verse:

"The world is reconciled and drowned out by the Spirit."[9]

* * *

Must we ask: Which spirit? The absolute Spirit of Hegel, who resided so long in Berlin? Or the spirit of the Christian Trinity, to whose sign Annette held fast? Or one of the many other spirits, which we are supposed to be able to tell apart? The poetic pantheism of Däubler encompasses them all with the same enthusiasm and pulls all of them into the stream of his rhythms. He can countenance it all. He can illuminate every word and every concept and let them ring out in limitless simultaneity. "Everything becomes a ball of unattempted dreams of rounding."[10] This poet lives with all religious and philosophical entities, just as the great Pan lives with all plants and animals. He surrounds himself by them [*lagert sich zu ihnen*], like Father Nile by his children in the famous ancient sculpture.[11] Yet a verse that stands on a gravestone does not remain in the realm of what is merely poetically detached. It ineluctably takes on something of a religious, metaphysical, or philosophical avowal and decision.

That verse about the spirit that reconciles the world is the last line in Däubler's great epic *Das Nordlicht* [*Northern Lights*]—its ending, its conclusion. The work itself is so full of life and soul that we need not detain ourselves here with polemical antitheses between spirit [*Geist*] and life, or between mind [*Geist*] and soul. This was clear to me from the beginning. But the actual historical–philosophical meaning of the symbol of the northern lights remained hidden to me for a long time. In a still very youthful work from the year 1916,[12] I gave a Christian interpretation, and Däubler, in his limitless generosity, received it without objection. Today I know that the northern lights shine in the pale glow of a gnosis of humanity. They are the meteorological symbol of a humanity that saves itself, an autochthonous radiation that is broadcast by the Prometheans [*Promethiden*] of the earth into the cosmos. The ideal–historical context in which Däubler's idea of the northern lights is to be understood first became clear to me as I came across an essay by Proudhon with a long commentary on the fate of the earth and its people. The French revolutionary, who was rich in ideas and loved such speculations, tells us that it is the fate of the earth gradually to freeze and, like the moon, to die. Humanity must then die with its planet, if it does not succeed in sublimating itself into Spirit—*Spiritualité, Conscience, Liberté*. For Däubler, the polar lights are the telluric witness and guarantor of just this salvation, by the Spirit and in the Spirit.

I found Proudhon's cosmic–historical–philosophical fantasy of the fate of the earth and its people in his art-philosophical essays, which appeared in book form in Paris in 1865.[13] It first fell into my hands in the year 1938, four years after Däubler's death, a full 28 years after I had begun my studies on the symbol of the northern lights; and in this context I had initially found some remarks by Charles Fourier and Gustave Flaubert. The mysterious hand that steers us as we reach for books led me to that passage in Proudhon and opened it for me quite late. I suspect that the Promethean idea of northern lights originated in Saint-Simonian circles. There in any case it would have acquired its ideal–historical virulence. How far Theodor Däubler was initiated into their esoterics is not known to me. His intuitive understanding of ancient mysteries was astounding, and the ancient mysteries have to do with sun, moon, Earth and stars. In this context—according to the writings of Plutarch, as discussed by Bachofen[14]—the soul is assigned to the moon, the mind to the sun, and the body to the earth. The northern lights are no ancient symbol of mysteries. Däubler knew and worked out a great deal [*unendlich Vieles*] from discussions, and also from apparently accidental phonetic encounters that gave his scent ever new nourishment. The *genius loci* of Florence, the unforeseeable effect of Bachofen and other sources of ideas of the nineteenth century captured him as well. He often made allusions to an esoteric knowledge but never spoke of the ideal–historical connections, whereas for me familiarity with the latter means access to knowledge.

The encounter with Proudhon's remark revealed to me the meaning of the northern lights symbol. I now recognized the origin of Däubler's concept of Spirit, which was nourished by metaphysical German springs, by esoteric Mediterranean cisterns, and by Promethean Atlantic Gulf Stream currents. Thus I became aware retrospectively of a slow development, over many years, that had distanced me internally from Däubler. Since 1910 I had placed myself with great eagerness in the service of his work. Fritz Eisler, with his great intelligence and tact, confirmed me in this. I dedicated the *Northern Lights* brochure of 1916 to Eisler's memory, after he was killed in September 1914 in France. From all that there emerged a heartfelt personal friendship with Däubler. After World War I it weakened. Däubler had made a name for himself [*sich durchgesetzt*]. Now Konrad Weiß, a Catholic Swabian, the poet of *The Sybil of Cumae* (1921), *Tantalus* (1929), and *The Christian Epimetheus* (1933),[15] drew closer to me. All of this took its course without partings or explanations, without options or decisions, without consultations or discussions, just as the grain of wood grows in a tree. It belongs to the lines of our life, which we can trace later but not foresee or determine in the midst of its development.

Konrad Weiß died in 1940 in Munich and is buried there. As for my own poor person, I have abandoned the hope of being buried in the mountains above the Mosel, in the land of my forefathers. But I still hope to find a grave in the Westphalian Sauerland, in the Catholic cemetery at Eiringhausen where my parents rest, above the Lenne—a river of the Sauerland that still carried beautiful, proud mountain waters in my childhood and that I've seen transformed into a poor canal for industrial waste in the course of my life. Yet I would not see it as a degradation if my bodily remains returned to the earth in the sand of the March Brandenburg, in anticipation of the Day of Judgment and resurrection of the dead. I will draft no epitaph. There should not even be a *hic et nunc* there. If, however, my child would like to know something of the secret [*arcanum*] in the fate of her father and asks me about words that touch the innermost core of my life, I can quote no verse of Däubler. I cannot answer in a Promethean way, rather only as a Christian Epimetheus, with a verse from Konrad Weiß:

So will the sense, the more it seeks itself,
From dark imprisonment the soul, [be] led to the world.
Accomplish what you must, it is already
Always achieved and you may only answer.[16]

For my daughter Anima Louise, on August 25, 1946

5

Ex captivitate salus

1

Our life acquires furrows and lines through our labors, through our productivity in work and profession. My home as teacher and researcher is in two areas of legal scholarship, international law and constitutional law. Both disciplines belong to public law. Work in these areas is about publicity in the strongest sense of the word. It concerns questions bearing upon domestic and foreign policy. Thus it is directly exposed to the danger of the political. The jurist in such fields cannot escape this danger, not even by disappearing into the nirvana of pure positivism. At best he can temper the danger either by establishing himself in remote borderlands, under historical or philosophical camouflage, or by developing the art of qualifications and obfuscations to the highest degree of perfection.

In quiet times neutral zones and comfortable parks are established for the protection of nature, intellect, and memorials. In troubled times this ceases. Then the danger immanent to all free thinking becomes acute. The researcher and teacher of public law suddenly finds himself pinned down and categorized as a result of any unguarded word and thought, and this by people who have never had an unguarded thought in their lives, to whom any freedom of the intellect is essentially foreign. But this is not all. The academic work of a scholar of public law, his writings themselves, place him in a particular country, among specific groups and powers, and in a particular time period. The material he assembles his concepts from and relies upon for his scholarly work binds him to political situations whose favor or disfavor, good or ill fortune, victory or defeat also encompasses the researcher and teacher and decides his personal fate.

This reality becomes most palpable in times of open or latent civil war. A civil war involves something particularly ghastly. It is a war between brothers, because it is fought within a common political entity that encompasses the opponent within one and the same legal order, and because both sides of the struggle simultaneously assert and deny this common political entity in absolute terms. Both place the opponent absolutely and unconditionally in the wrong. They suspend the rights of the opponent, but they do so in the name of justice. Submission to this jurisprudence [*Jurisdiktion*] of the enemy[1] belongs in the essence of civil war. Thus civil war has a narrow, specifically dialectical relation to law. It cannot be other than righteous in the sense of being self-righteous and becomes in this way the ur-type or prototype of righteous and self-righteous war.

More dangerously than in any other kind of war, each party is forced ruthlessly to presuppose its own rightness and, just as ruthlessly, the wrongness of the opponent. One side asserts a legal right, the other a natural right. The former confers a right to obedience, the latter a right of resistance. The interference of legal reasoning and institutions poisons the struggle. It makes the conflict escalate to the most extreme severity insofar as it transforms the means and methods of the judiciary into means and methods of annihilation. One sits in judgment without ceasing to be an enemy. The establishment of revolutionary tribunals and people's courts is not intended to diminish the terror but rather to sharpen it. The public, legal defamations and discriminations, the public or secret blacklists, the acts of declaring individuals enemies of the state, of the people, or of humanity do not mean granting the opponent the legal position of an enemy in the sense of a belligerent party. On the contrary, they are supposed to deprive him even of this last right. They amount to a total disenfranchisement in the name of the law. The enmity becomes so absolute that even the age-old sacral distinction between enemy and criminal dissolves in the paroxysm of self-righteousness. Doubt about one's own righteousness [*Recht*] counts as treason; interest in the opponent's reasoning is perfidiousness; and an attempt at discussion becomes consorting with the enemy.

All these are expressions and manifestations of the dialectical relation between civil war and law. There are different kinds of war. There are holy wars, just wars, and wars as duel [*Duellkriege*]. The holy war and the war as duel both retain something of the original character of a judgment of God. The just war, in contrast, places judgment in the hands of human beings. In the age of modern positivism, justice is transformed into a law made by people for people. It makes of law a settlement of settlements [*eine Setzung von Setzungen*]. To the same degree it deprives just war of the last vestiges of a sacral thought. The goddess of justice opens Pandora's box, and there appear not only the snares of intricate trials but also the judicially clothed terrors of bloody civil wars.

2

What becomes of legal scholarship in this tragic dialectic of law? What becomes of the legal scholar if every potentate turns into a pitiless dogmatist?

In terms of great and heroic world history, this difficult question is easy to answer. In the twelfth and thirteenth centuries the spirit of Roman law was born anew out of terrible partisan struggles in the cities of middle and upper Italy. In the confessional civil wars of the sixteenth century names such as those of John Story on the Catholic side and Donellus on the Protestant side shine forth among those persecuted and expelled. The church has now given us a patron saint in Thomas More. I will speak later of the founders of public law, of *ius publicum Europaeum*. Since their era, the age of heroes, of course, the jurists have been thoroughly officialized and absorbed into the bourgeoisie. In the nineteenth century the risks of their profession seemed to grow even smaller than those of other occupations. Viewed in this way, the response of the larger history of the world is rather simple. Briefly stated, it runs as follows: times change; in bad times, many perish; a few become martyrs and even saints; and, out of suffering and adversity, new generations draw the motivation for new achievements.

This response is cruel and comforting at the same time. It bears the double countenance that all answers and oracles of the Hegelian World Spirit carry. We know this. World history is not the soil of happiness. We do not wish to scorn its comfort, but this comfort is summary and sweeping. The sufferings that human beings bring upon one another are terrible. We cannot simply turn away from them. But how are we to bear the sight of them? How, in particular, should a person for whom knowledge about right has become a part of his existence bear the naked fact, indeed the bare possibility of a total disenfranchisement, regardless of whom it strikes in individual cases? And if it strikes him personally, then the situation of the disenfranchised jurist, of the *lawyer* declared an *outlaw*,[2] of the legal expert placed *hors-la-loi* in fact acquires an especially bitter supplement [*Zusatz*] on top of all the other physical and psychic ordeals, a thorn of knowledge that inflames the burning wound ever anew.

> Great, oh gods, are your gifts
> but the pain that accompanies them
> weighs all too heavily upon me.[3]

3

The last asylum of the person tormented by other human beings is always a prayer, a prayer cried out [*Stoßgebet*] to the crucified God. In the shearing of pain [*Schur des Schmerzens*][4] we recognize Him and He recognizes us. Our God was not stoned by Jews as a Jew and was not beheaded by Romans as a Roman. He could not be beheaded. He no longer had a head in the legal sense, because he no longer had any rights. He died by crucifixion, the death of a slave imposed upon him by a foreign conqueror.

Sometimes the doors of our captivity suddenly open, and a mysterious path appears. It leads inward, to many forms of silence and stillness, but also to new encounters and to a new present. As long as our consciousness remains bound to the labors of our earthly existence, a new connection with the past emerges from this, a personal coexistence with the thinkers whose situation corresponds to our own. There emerge contacts and conversations whose power moves the mountains of entire libraries and whose fire consumes the false authenticity of enormous piles of material. Souls and spirits speak to us personally, of us and of themselves. Here I do not mean the genies and spirits of the Renaissance and of humanism; I mean no Parnassus and no Olympus—also not the foaming goblet of the world of spirits from which the philosophy of German idealism thought to imbibe eternity. All of this is not my subject. I have poor, suffering people in mind, people in a solitary position of danger akin to my own and whose thought remains in this place, so that I may understand it well and may be sure that they understand me.

My work is dedicated to the scholarly clarification of public law. This is an area that extends far beyond the borders of a nation, and certainly beyond the positive legality of a generation. It is, nevertheless, not an unsituated generality or an undifferentiated matter pertaining to the entire world and to all ages. It is a creation of the European intellect, a *ius publicum Europaeum*, and remains bound to a particular epoch. It emerged in the sixteenth and seventeenth centuries from appalling European civil wars. This is its beginning and its *principium* [principle/beginning]. In this initial situation lies its relationship with the situation of our present time, an intellectual relationship that is more than an historical parallel—and also more than an analogy and something other than what Oswald Spengler termed a homology. There are identities of intellectual existence that extend even to the most personal destinies, even into the souls of all those who, with their thought and their concepts, strive to master such a situation intellectually and must bear the entire burden of this endeavor.

4

Some teachers of public law from the sixteenth and seventeenth centuries, the period of emergence of *ius publicum Europaeum*, became so famous that their fame itself has its own history, and thus offers an interesting theme for intellectual–historical observation. Francisco de Vitoria, Alberico Gentili, and Hugo Grotius belong here. I know them, their work, their lives and their fates, also the history of their fame up to the present day. I love them. They belong without a doubt to our *camp*.[5] However, they do not belong in my barracks room. In immediate proximity to me are two others, who founded the law of nations upon the constitutional law of states: Jean Bodin and Thomas Hobbes.

These two names from the era of confessional civil wars have come to be, for me, names of living contemporaries, names of brothers with whom I have grown into a family across the centuries. For 30 years, the mysterious hand that steers us as we reach for books has had me open their books again and again, and each time at passages heavy with meaning; that was back then, before my library was taken away from me. Today I am forced to rely upon my memory. But the thoughts and formulations of both these figures are just as familiar to me as the thought and speech of a brother. They have kept my thinking alert and driven it forward when the positivism of my generation weighed down upon me and a blind need for security sought to paralyze me. In them I have found more topical answers to the questions of my time in international and constitutional law than in the commentaries on the Bismarckian or Weimar constitutions, or in the publications of the Geneva League of Nations. They stand closer to me than all the positivists of the status quo specific to these particular façades of legality. For this reason I would like to dwell on them here for a moment.

Both were entirely formed by civil wars. But they are as different from each other as two human individuals could possibly be. Bodin is an eager legalist, sometimes too eager and somewhat humorless. He is very erudite, both as a jurist of the school of Bartolus and as a humanist of the school of Jacques Cujas, but he stays within the limits of his practical profession. From this position he approaches economic, philosophical, and theological questions. He often ventures into the line of fire of the domestic policy of his country and of his time, gets involved in perilous situations, finds himself in mortal danger and changes over to the wrong side at the wrong moment, shortly before his death. In this way he undid the practical gains of his life's work. He is neutral in the hopeless dogfight of theological argument. He sees what is specifically political between the two parties of the confessional civil war as residing in a conciliatory neutrality and tolerance. From the impulse for public peace, security, and order there emerge, in his head, the first juridically clear concepts of European constitutional law. He becomes the first modern critic of religion and of the Bible. But in his own person he remains pious and devout to the point of superstition, so that the dogmatism of the contending theologians fails to make belief altogether too difficult for him. He believes in witches and demons and even has a secret protective spirit, a *spiritus familiaris*, who warns him about murderers and protects him from them. He delineated the decisive concept of *ius publicum Europaeum*, that of the domestically and internationally sovereign state, with incomparable success. He is one of the midwives of the modern state. But he did not yet grasp the modern Leviathan that appears in four shapes, the fourfold combination of God, animal, person, and machine. His desperation was not overwhelming enough for this.

Hobbes, by contrast, understood it all the better. After a further century of theological conflicts and European civil wars, his desperation was infinitely deeper than Bodin's. Hobbes was one of the great solitary figures of the seventeenth century, all of whom knew one another. He grasped not only the fourfold essence of the modern Leviathan but also how to deal with it, as well as the behavior advisable for an independently thinking individual who engages with such a dangerous theme. For Hobbes, the political is no longer neutrality but the clear delimitation made by the line of friendship. He already lives in the age of the *amity line*,[6] the age of successful pirates and buccaneers. He thought, spoke, and wrote about these dangerous things in the inalienable freedom of the intellect and always with good personal cover, always either on the run or from some inconspicuous concealment. He was no practitioner and no public figure, and not once did he personally expose himself. At the private personal level as well, he remained aware of the basis of all law; and, for him, this was the mutual relationship that results from protection and obedience. On this point the man without illusions was even less susceptible than usual to being deceived. He went to those places where he could count on the cessation of civil war and find effective protection. He did not envisage running onto the knives of the rulers and dogmatists of his age. Thus he secured his observation post and achieved a systematic construction of the most lucid conceptual coherence. He lived, in fear and caution, beyond the age of 90 and led the life of an independent mind. From him as from Bodin there came strong impulses for religious and biblical critique. But, while Bodin remained theologically pious and even superstitious, Hobbes is already a figure of the Enlightenment and an agnostic.

One should not speak too much of one's friends. Each of these two is my friend, different as they may be in other respects: one so pious and superstitious, the other so disenchanted and Enlightenment-oriented. And I do not deny myself a prayer for their souls. Jean Bodin, who himself prayed so much and so fervently, would take it for granted. He would be amazed if I did not. But Thomas Hobbes would hardly think ill of me either. He renounced speaking of such things, but was in favor of prayer when it really leads to peace. The civil war stoked by theologians and sectarians drove him to despair. Nevertheless he was not an Enlightener in the style of the eighteenth century, not to speak of the nineteenth. His Enlightenment is not yet arrogant. It is a bitter fruit, plucked in fear and worry, the fruit of an age of confessional civil war and murderous dogmatism.

5

Sometimes, in our deepest humiliation, we are suddenly struck by pride in our godly origins. That is a blissful moment. Not a dream or a childhood memory and no paradise, but rather an image of the most intensive copresence of centuries of historical efforts, in which we ourselves feature, with our poor life's work. We hear the contents of the discussions of an entire epoch in simple, clear words, and see our own reality in a moment of concrete localization

Ex captivitate salus

and triangulation [*Angulierung*]. A single second teaches us where we actually are, where we come from, and where our path of suffering is going. I want to try to speak of one such moment, although I know that I cannot reproduce the image of instantaneous copresence. I must lay it out discursively, in strands [*Linien*] from the history of ideas and the sociology of knowledge, and must translate its words into a language entirely different from that of an immediate simultaneity.

We are aware of jurisprudence as a specifically European phenomenon. It is neither just practical intelligence nor only a handcraft. It is deeply enmeshed in the adventure of western rationalism. It comes as spirit from a noble parentage. Its father is the reborn Roman law, its mother the Roman church. Separation from the mother was finally completed after many centuries of difficult dispute in the age of confessional civil war. The child held to the father, Roman law, and left the mother's home. It sought a new house and found it in the state. The new home was princely, a palace of the Renaissance or the Baroque. Jurists felt proud and far superior to theologians.

This is how *ius publicum Europaeum* emerged from the confessional civil wars of the sixteenth and seventeenth centuries. At its beginning stands an antitheological slogan, a call for silence that a founder of modern international law directs to the theologians: *Silete, theologi, in munere alieno!* ["Keep quiet, theologians, on alien territory (*sc.* on matters outside your remit)!"]. This is what Albericus Gentilis shouted against them, on the matter of the just war debate.[7] I still hear him shout today.

The jurists' withdrawal from the church was no secession to a holy mountain, rather the reverse: an exodus from a holy mountain to the realm of the profane. On leaving, the jurists took some holy trappings [*Heiligtümer*] with them, whether openly or secretly. The state decorated itself with some simulacra of ecclesiastical ancestry. The power of earthly princes was augmented by attributes and arguments of spiritual descent. The jurists of *ius publicum Europaeum* came into positions that had been occupied by theologians until that time. They inherited something of the *potestas spiritualis* [spiritual domain] of the Christian church of the Middle Ages. In long disputes with worldly rulers, medieval clerics had developed well-considered doctrines of just war and just resistance against tyrants. They formulated [*fanden*] sentences of such indestructible currency that one can only cite them in Latin, such as the great chapter titles of *Policraticus*:[8] *tyrannum licet adulari* ["one is allowed to praise a tyrant"]; *tyrannum licet decipere* ["one is allowed to deceive a tyrant"]; *tyrannum licet occidere* ["one is allowed to kill a tyrant"]. The sequence speaks for itself.

These theologians of the Christian Middle Ages passed on to later and very different periods the ancient designations for an enemy of the human species: *hostis publicus* and *hostis generis humani*. But with such teachings and concepts they were firmly on the ground and within the institutions of a well-organized system of *auctoritas*, even of *potestas spiritualis*. They were themselves, with their entire existence, bearers of the *potestas spiritualis* of the Roman church. Their doctrines of the right of resistance, of just war, and of tyrannicide were, in terms of their significance, not instruments of civil war but rather of an existing, recognized, superior ordering power, which by no means shirked its duty to preserve order.

This was lost with the separation from the Roman church. Nevertheless, the jurists of public law developed further the doctrines and concepts of the sovereign state. Thus they succeeded in purifying the doctrine of just war from the elements of civil war, insofar as they separated the question of *iusta causa belli* [the just cause of war] from that of *iustus hostis* [the just enemy] and restored awareness of the old distinction between enemy and criminal. That was their great achievement and became the core of a new international law: *ius publicum Europaeum*.

These jurists revealed themselves to be protectors of their own tradition. They formed their own order [*Stand*] with at least an intellectual authority, if not a spiritual one. They were not just technical specialists at the disposal of the potentates and dogmatists of their age. In this way they found themselves in a dangerous in-between position. They eliminated the influence of theologians and freed themselves from religious institutions. Thus they joined the side of the Enlightenment and of progress. Yet they remained protectors of their own tradition and authority, and in this sense they were conservative. Their authority was secularized, but still far from being profane. When they carried the holy trappings from the church into the state, they did not intend to profane and destroy these symbols; they wanted to save what could be saved from the fury of the confessional civil war. They did not mean to steal from the church; they thought only of rescuing precious articles. But we know what happens with rescues. Their intention was good and honorable, though the historical repercussions took a different course. The jurists were rationalists, but not in the sense defined by the subsequent centuries and not in the sense of positivism and of pure technicity.

The two great founders of public law, Bodin and Hobbes, are outstanding figures and bearers of this transformation of a *potestas spiritualis* and of an intermediate position. Both are in bitter conflict with the theologians. Both emerged from this conflict to become the most effective founders of a religious and biblical critique. Nevertheless, both hold to the belief of their forebears, and not merely in a superficial way. They did not go over to the state out of arrogance, but rather out of desperation, when they saw that the dogmatism of theologians and sectarians stoked the civil war anew. The thought never occurred to them to ground a new religion, certainly not one of secularism and positivism. Thus arose their intermediate position. They stood between the very old and the very new and were therefore reviled and defamed from both sides. To the theologians, they were atheists; to the radical philosophers of the Enlightenment, they were merely opportunistic hypocrites. Victor Hugo, the great figurehead [*Großkophta*] of secularism, called poor Bodin a crocodile. Hobbes was considered the prophet of the Leviathan and for this reason was infamous and ostracized even back then, since most people are far too primitive to distinguish a diagnostician from a prophet.

The intermediate position was not limited to antagonism between the Christian confessions, to Rome and Geneva. It expanded and deepened into an antagonism between tradition and revolution—and did not stop even there. Its ultimate significance was the alternative of a complete profanation. Of course this did not become clear so quickly, since an intermediate epoch of liberalization intervened, a time of fabulous prosperity that could easily afford the luxury of conservative feelings and attitudes. During this epoch things went very well for the jurists. They now lived only part of the time in the house of the state. The better situated ones were quartered in society, no longer in a palace but in an even more comfortable hotel. The holy trappings faded away by comparison to philosophical or historical jewelry. Yet they were still of antiquarian or decorative interest, and in the great hotel there was also room for certain traditions, robes, and wigs. It was the consistently technical age that first eliminated them and completed the profanation without remainder. This age laid bare with inexorable logic where jurisprudence stands, namely between theology and technique, and placed the jurists before a difficult choice, in that it immersed them in the new objectivity of pure technicity. The traditional holy trappings now become non-objective and old-fashioned. Instead of a comfortable hotel, the bunkers and barracks of the technical age open up. Now it is the jurists who receive a call to silence. Now it is to them—should there still be enough Latin—that the technicians of potentates and dogmatists can shout: *Silete jurisconsulti!* ["Keep quiet, lawyers!"]

These are two remarkable calls for silence at the beginning and at the end of an epoch. At the beginning lies a call for silence that emanates from jurists and is directed at the theologians of just war. At the end lies a demand, directed at jurists, for pure—in other words completely profane—technicity. I do not wish to discuss here the connection between the two orders of silence. It is merely good and salutary to recall that the situation was no less brutal at the beginning of the epoch than it is at its end. Every situation has its secret, and every scholarly discipline bears its secret [*arcanum*] within itself. I am the last knowing representative of *ius publicum Europaeum*, its last teacher and researcher in an existential sense, and I experience its ending as did Benito Cereno the journey of the pirate ship. Silence is appropriate to this place and time. We need not fear it. By being silent we reflect upon ourselves and upon our godly origins.

6

I have spoken of myself here, actually for the first time in my life. A person who thinks in a scholarly way prefers to speak of factual matters. A researcher who makes historical observations sees himself in the framework and in the waves of historical forces and powers—in church, state, party, class, profession, and generation. A jurist who has trained himself and many others to objectivity evades psychological self-portrayals. The tendency to literary confession is spoiled for me by ugly examples such as those of Jean Jacques Rousseau and poor August Strindberg. As an expert in constitutional law, however, I have a highly interesting fellow sufferer [*Schicksalsbruder*] *in constitutionalibus* [in constitutional matters], one who has achieved astounding feats in personal reports and confessions: Benjamin Constant, the protagonist of the doctrine of liberal constitutionalism. He was not only a brilliant constructor of constitutions but also the author of the first psychological novel, *Adolphe*,[9] as well as of a surprising *journal intime* and countless letters. I find him more likeable than the two self-tormenters just mentioned. Yet not even his example could bring me to literary confessions. Whoever wishes to confess, go and present yourself to the priest.

In any case, today we have to answer enough questions for ourselves, which are posed by the most disparate parties. The reason for questioning is usually to call us into question—our very selves and our existence. I am not speaking here of agencies and offices that ask us all manner of things that do not relate to our essence but concern merely points of attribution for liabilities and detentions. Nor am I speaking of the questions posed to us as one would set snares and traps. This sort of thing still belongs in part to the realm of the old Leviathan, which I know well; it is in part the hunting ground of the head forester we know through Ernst Jünger.[10] How a person is supposed to behave in the position of hounded game is a sad problem in itself. I will say no more of it.

What I say here is intended neither as a form of journalism nor as an apology. It belongs neither on the street nor on the stage, neither in the forum nor upon the lectern. I speak because I want to send word to a few deceased friends, while I, for one, am still in the clutches of this earthly life; because I want to give a sign to some living friends from whom I am separated and to loyal students in all countries; and, finally, because I think of my daughter Anima and my godchild Carl Alexander. Speaking with them violates no secret [*arcanum*]. We are all bound together by the stillness of silence and the inalienable secret of the godly origins of humanity.

Summer 1946

6

Wisdom of the Cell

You wish to perceive yourself and (perhaps even more) your real situation? There is a good touchstone for this. Try to notice which of the thousands of definitions of the human being seems immediately clear to you.

I attend to this in my cell, and it becomes immediately clear to me that the human being is naked. At his most naked is the person unclothed before someone clothed, disarmed before someone armed, powerless before someone in power. Adam and Eve already knew all this upon their eviction from the Garden of Eden.

The question immediately arises: On whom must the definition of the human be modeled, on the naked or on the dressed person? On the disarmed or on the armed? On the powerless or on the powerful? And which of the two is closer to paradise? In the paradises of this world today people move about in clothes. It is immediately clear to me that I am naked.

"Now you stand naked, naked as at birth, in desolate expanses."[1]

In the desolate expanses of a narrow cell. The articles of clothing left for me confirm only the objective nakedness.

They even underline it in a highly ironic and uncomfortably emphatic way. You see yourself thrown back upon your self and upon your last reserves. What are my last reserves? A remainder of physical force. This is of course easy to extinguish. Nevertheless, at the moment it is still here. I see clearly in an instant:

> I inherited only
> my own body,
> and that I waste away as I live.[2]

This line is sung by Richard Wagner's Siegfried in a wonderful, rising and falling interval. A bubbling, physical feeling of happiness seems to be captured here. No later musician or lyricist expressed so much physical joy. The force of this artistic expression still obviously rides the waves ridden by the Revolution of 1848 in Germany. The musical interval comes from Richard Wagner. The line itself, though, can be traced to Max Stirner.[3] With this we approach a paradise in which something of paradisiacal nakedness shines forth.

* * *

I have known Max Stirner since *Unterprima* [the eighth year of German secondary school]. It is thanks to this acquaintanceship that I was prepared for some of what I have encountered to this day, which might otherwise have surprised me. Whoever knows the depths of the European train of thought between 1830 and 1848 is prepared for most of what rings loud in the world today. Since 1848 the rubble field left by the self-decomposition of German theology and idealistic philosophy has changed into a force field of theogonic and cosmogonic approaches. What explodes today was

prepared before 1848. The fire that burns today was laid at
that time. There are certain uranium mines in the history of
ideas. Among them are the Presocratics, a few fathers of the
church, and also a few writings from the period before 1848.
Poor Max definitely belongs here.

Taken as a whole, he is awful, loutish, pretentious,
self-important [*renommistisch*], a Pennalist,[4] a degenerate
student, a lump [*Knote*], an egomaniac, clearly a serious psy-
chopath. He crows in a loud, unpleasant voice: I am Me, I
care about nothing but Myself [*Mir geht nichts über Mich*].
His verbal sophisms are unbearable. The hep cat [*Zazou*]
of his cigar-smoking, basement-bar bohemian lifestyle
[*Stammtisch-Bohème*] is disgusting. But Max knows something very important. He knows that the *I* is no object of
thought. And so he came up with the most beautiful, in any
case the most German book title in the whole of German
literature: *Der Einzige und sein Eigentum* [*The Ego and Its
Own*].[5] At this moment, Max is the only person who visits
me in my cell. This touches me deeply, as he is such a rabid
egoist.

He expressed his ultimate motivation in a letter in which
he says: then we will become once again like the animals
in the woods and the flowers of the field. This is the real
yearning of this egomaniac. This is the new paradise. This is
nature and the natural law, the suspension of self-alienation
and of self-externalization in a problem-free corporeality
[*Leibhaftigkeit*]: the Adamitic happiness of the garden of
earthly delights, which Hieronymous Bosch cast in white
nakedness upon a panel;[6] also the animals in the woods and
the flowers of the field; the flight of the midge in sunshine; the
completely natural nature and the natural law of the deepest
spheres of telluric existence; the utterly unencumbered

twittering of Rossini's thieving magpie;[7] the pure identitfi-
cation with oneself in the pleasurable feeling of a blissfully
accelerated bloodstream. Pan awakens and appears in the
earth-conscious circle [*erdbewußten Kreis*].[8] Max is one of
the first Panists who later peopled the field of German literature and the paradises of its deproblematization.

But this poor Pan was not equal to the challenge of
modern natural science. Today his happiness is not even
an illusion any longer. It is the pleasure of the poor holi-
daymaker escaped from the big city into the countryside,
the fleeting awakening of cheerful feelings in the holiday
child—or, for that matter, the blissful feeling of a poetry
award winner. Their desire is no longer for eternity. It moves
within the frame of a right to vacation. It still naturally
creates an appetite for more, but submits itself, in resigna-
tion, to the fact that the vacation cannot be eternal. This
poor ego can only wed itself to its echo; and in this infertile,
self-indulgent marriage it is no longer lonely [*vereinsamt*]
but by now organizationally appropriated [*vereinnahmt*].
Planning has appropriated it long ago.

The plan appears and Pan stops smirking. Pan sinks, the
plan appears on the scene [*der Plan tritt auf den Plan*]. A nice
example of the immanent oracular character of our German
language.

* * *

New paradises beckon now: this time the paradises of a
thoroughly planned world, with all the glories of unchained
forces of production and a power of consumption increased
to infinity, as well as with generously extended leisure time,
endowed with the appropriate recreational activities. It is
the paradise of a technicized earth and its thoroughly organ-

ized humanity. The natural barrier falls; the limits of society capture us in its place. They not only capture us, they change us. The matter is not one of recognizing the world and the human being any more, but rather of changing them.

For 10 years we have occasionally seen how quickly the artificial paradises of technology change into real hells. We learned this lesson especially clearly in the cold winter of 1946/7 in Berlin, as burst pipes destroyed the wastewater system and the downside of paradise became visible. But these are disruptions that can be avoided. Also, they impact just the vanquished. One only needs to find and isolate the source of the trouble, the disrupter, and the problem is solved. We will find the disrupter. The disrupter is the guilty party and the guilty party is the disrupter. Who this is in each concrete case will be communicated to us by the responsible agencies. We will nevertheless reach the goal of technology.

We? Fifty years ago our progressive grandparents told us: in 50 years *we* will fly. In fact flight is a reality today. But neither our long-deceased grandparents nor we, their grandchildren, may fly. Not we, but others fly. This *we* of our progressive grandparents had something touching about it. It rested on a naïve identification with the masters of the world, who would be supported by technical means in 50 years' time and whose wishes the unleashed productive forces would fulfill. All myths of progress are based upon such identifications, that is, upon the childlike assumption that one will be among the gods of the new paradise. In reality, however, the selection process is very rigorous, and the new elites take care to keep a sharper watch than the old. We should thus pause before growing enthusiastic about the new paradise. One cannot reasonably say more today.

Perhaps in 50 or 100 years humans will be free of misery;
those who live today, in any case. The others will no longer
interest themselves in our current misery. For this reason we
do not intend either to chase after them or to run ahead of
them. I am only interested for the moment in whether the
human being in the new paradise of technology is naked or
clothed. The clothing industry will probably undergo such an
upswing and unleash such productive forces that *we* will be
able to afford new, fantastic costumes daily. Charles Fourier
may paint this in detail. The prophesy of Vergil's Fourth
Eclogue, that the wool of lambs will grow in the most
beautiful purple all by itself,[9] then, seems old-fashioned
and indeed reactionary. But perhaps our dream of fantastic
quantities of incessantly new clothing is itself old-fashioned
and reactionary. Perhaps there will be no clothes and costumes at all. Technology will advance so far that we will
be able to wrap ourselves in envelopes of light and warmth.
Wonderful. Yet there is more. We will transform even the
material of our body into radiation. This is, then, the technically transfigured body, just as our pilots are the technically
perfected angels. *We*—that is, then, only the select few of the
new paradise, of course: the new elite.

Hence they are neither naked nor clothed. The distinction
loses its sense in a new stage of being [*Daseinstufe*]. They are
no longer humans at all; they are the entirely other. A few
theologians today say that God would be the entirely other.
But what is entirely other is entirely unpredictable. Why
should the new man not be the entirely other? The human
being, as we know it, is something that has to be overcome.
Why should it not be overcome in this way? It will then be
no longer procreated, no longer conceived, and no longer
born. Then Aldous Huxley's brave new world,[10] with its

consistent, highly scientific planning of offspring, becomes obsolete as well; and so does our question about the definition of the human being. Everything, then, is just radiation.

Am I on this earth for the purpose of working so that technology may transform us into radiation? If so, under whose authority should I place myself in order to take up the work? For I have long ceased to exist for myself, alone and in isolation; I have long been organizationally appropriated.

These are questions it is no longer permissible even to ask. You have nothing more to ask, rather only answer the questions posed to you. Not we, but others formulate the questionnaires that call you and your questions into question. Understand at last what this means. It is tasteless of you to use the luxury of solitary confinement to indulge in the illusion that you are only isolated and not thoroughly appropriated by now.

Do you want to succumb once again to deception?

* * *

Self-delusion is inherent to loneliness. The solitary person thinks with himself and talks to himself, and in talking to ourselves, as we know, we are talking to a dangerous flatterer. The moralists were right to consider autobiography a sign of vanity. Yet vanity would still be the most harmless and endearing of the motives under consideration here. The saints write no autobiographies. At the deepest core of the cell lie the internal dialogue and the self-delusion.

Terrible is the fear of Descartes, who philosophizes at the stove in his lonely room and thinks only of escaping the evil, deceptive spirit, *spiritus malignus*, against whose tricks we are never secure—and least of all when we feel secure. In fear of deception, Descartes becomes a masked man, *l'homme au masque.* He is no longer naked, but no longer clothed either. He is masked. *Larvatus prodeo* ["I advance wearing a mask"]. Fear is all the more terrible as it becomes the source of ever new deceptions. Whoever thinks of escaping the deception runs headlong into it. Deception of feeling and of the understanding, deception of the flesh and of the mind, deception of vice and of virtue, deception of man and woman.

I always succumb to deception again and again. I have escaped it again and again. I will also succeed with the final leap. Come, beloved death.

* * *

Death can betray us as well. Both death as a leap into the realm of freedom and the heath/ens' soft death. All deception is and remains self-deception. The self-armoring of Max Stirner is the highest self-deception. It is for this reason that his mixture of harmlessness and cunning, of honest challenge and deceitful swindle is so ugly. Like any egomaniac, he sees the enemy in the *not-I.* Thus the whole world becomes his enemy, and he imagines that it would have to fall for him if, remaining free, he were to offer it the brotherly kiss. In this way he hides from the dialectical power of ego splitting and seeks to elude the enemy by means of deception. But the enemy is an objective power. He will not escape it, and the real enemy will not let itself be deceived.

Who is my enemy, then? Is my enemy the person who feeds me here, in the cell? He even clothes and shelters me. The cell is the clothing he donates. I ask myself, then: Who can my enemy be? To be sure, I do it in such a way as to be able to acknowledge him as enemy, and in fact it must be acknowledged that he acknowledges me as enemy. In this mutual acknowledgment of acknowledgment lies the greatness of the concept. It is not very appropriate for an age of the masses with pseudo-theological enemy myths. What is more, the theologians tend to define the enemy as something that must be destroyed. But I am a jurist, not a theologian.

Whom in the world can I acknowledge as my enemy? Clearly only him who can call me into question. By recognizing him as enemy I acknowledge that he can call me into question. And who can really call me into question? Only I myself. Or my brother. The other proves to be my brother, and the brother proves to be my enemy. Adam and Eve had two sons, Cain and Abel. Thus begins the history of humankind. This is what the father of all things looks like. This is the dialectical tension that keeps world history moving, and world history has not yet ended.

Take care, then, and do not speak lightly of the enemy. One categorizes oneself through one's enemy. One grades oneself through what one recognizes as hostility. The destroyers, who justify themselves by claiming that the destroyers must be destroyed, are of course bad. But all destruction is only self-destruction. The enemy, by contrast, is the other. Remember the great sentences of the philosopher: the relation in the other to itself, that is the real infinity. The negation of the negation, says the philosopher, is no neutralization, rather the real infinite depends upon it. But the real infinite is the basic concept of his philosophy.

"The enemy is our own question as form."[11]

Woe to him who has no *friend*, for his enemy will sit in judgment upon him.

Woe to him who has no *enemy*, for *I* will be his enemy on Judgment Day.

* * *

This is the wisdom of the cell. I lose my time and win my space. Suddenly the calm that holds the meaning of the words overcomes [*übereilt*] me. *Space* [*Raum*] and *Rome* [*Rom*] are the same word. Wonderful are the spatial force [*Raumkraft*] and the germinal force [*Keimkraft*] of the German language. It has brought about the rhyme between word and place. It has even preserved the spatial sense of the word rhyme [*Reim*] and allowed its poets the dark play between rhyme [*Reim*] and home [*Heimat*].

In rhyme the word seeks the filial sound of its meaning. The German rhyme is not the beacon [*Leuchtfeuer*] of the rhymes of Victor Hugo. It is echo, clothing, and decoration and at the same time a divining rod for the location of meaning. Now I am seized by the word of sybilline poets, my dissimilar friends Theodor Däubler and Konrad Weiß. The dark play of their rhymes becomes meaning and appeal.

I listen for their word, I listen and suffer and understand that I am not naked but rather clothed, and on the way to a house. I see the defenseless, rich fruit of the years, the defenseless rich fruit from which meaning springs by right [*aus der dem Recht der Sinn erwächst*].[12]

> Echo grows before each word;
> like a storm from the open place
> it hammers through our gate.[13]

April 1947

7

Song of the 60-Year-Old

I have lived through destiny pulling on the reins [*die Escavessaden*[1] *des Schicksals*],
Victories and defeats, revolutions and restorations,
Inflations and deflations, bombardments,
Defamations, regime changes and burst pipes,
Hunger and cold, camp and solitary confinement.
Through all of this I have passed,
And all has passed through me.

I know the many forms of terror,
Terror from above and terror from below,
Terror on land and terror from the air,
Terror legal and extralegal,
Brown, red, and checkered terror,
And the worst, which no one dares to name.
I know them all and I know their grip.

I know the megaphones of power and of law,
The amplifiers and meaning distorters of the regime,
The blacklists with many names,
And the card files of the persecutors.

What should I now sing? The hymn *Placebo*?[2]
Should I unproblematically envy the plants and the animals?
Quake in panic in the circle of Panists?
In the bliss of the midge that bobs in [*die nach innen hüpft*]?

Three times have I sat in the belly of the fish.
I looked in the eye death at the hands of the hangman.
Yet the word of sybilline poets surrounded me protectively
And a saint from the East redemptively opened the door for
      me.

Son of this consecration, shiver not—
Hark and suffer!

June 11, 1948
CS

Appendix

Foreword to the Spanish Edition

As Germany lay on the ground, defeated, in early 1945, not only the Russians but also the Americans undertook mass internments and defamed entire categories of the German population. The Americans termed their method "automatic arrest." This means that thousands and hundreds of thousands of members of certain demographic groups—for example all high-level civil servants—were summarily [*ohne jede weitere Rücksicht*] stripped of their rights and taken to a camp. This was the logical result of the criminalization of an entire people and the completion of the infamous Morgenthau Plan.

I was in such a camp under automatic arrest in 1945/6. In March 1947 I came to be held for two months in the prison at Nuremberg, as witness and "possible defendant," as this interesting institution of American criminal proceedings is known, which allows witnesses to be preemptively incarcerated. Neither in automatic arrest nor during this time in prison or at any later point was any formal charge lodged against me. Nor was any punishable action proven. But it was precisely this experience of modern methods of criminalization, the concrete encounter with the results of a doctrine of just war, that had to make the deepest impression upon an expert and teacher of law in general and of international law in particular.

Most of the pieces printed here were written under automatic arrest, in the camp at Berlin-Lichterfelde-Süd, a camp that was very tough in the winter of 1945/6 and where there was a strict ban on writing. Nevertheless there was a humane American camp doctor who, out of sympathy, allowed me to make notes and even helped me via evasion of controls to get letters and notes out of the camp. It is chiefly thanks to his contribution that this little book came out, and thus he must be named here. His first name was Charles; he came from Boston; his education and humanity rescued America's honor in our eyes. His understanding and his heart had remained free of the psychosis created by a horrible war propaganda. It goes without saying that the American camp administrations of that time soon removed him from his post. But he had done his providential work. I do not know what became of him. May God protect and bless him wherever he is today.

I ask my reader to read this book as if it were a series of letters personally directed to him. Only in this way is the form of exposition justified and understandable. This book emerges from a mass situation characteristic of modern methods of warfare. This is not a case of romantic or heroic prison literature, of complaints or outpourings in the style of Silvio Pellico's *Le mie prigioni*,[1] of individualistic lyrical confessions like Paul Verlaine's *Mes prisons*,[2] or even of *The Ballad of Reading Gaol* by Oscar Wilde.[3] Today the all-conquering progress of modern technology forces a new form of severity and cruelty, a hard and cruel coldness that manifests itself not only in the modern invention of the Cold

War. The progress of modern technology is at the same time progress in the removal of romantic subjectivism, progress in the appropriation of the human individual, progress in mass criminalization and mass automation. A giant apparatus indiscriminately swallows up hundreds of thousands of people. The old Leviathan appears almost cozy by comparison, and the old prison almost idyllic.

If the victim of such machinery speaks, this is not so much a matter of saying how one feels as one of saying what one thinks under the pressures of such a situation. All the dignity of the human being is concentrated in thinking. The situation induced by the pressure of automation is so strong that any mere aphorism becomes unimportant. But also any systematics grows weak, insofar as it emerged from other situations. I ask that this book be read as a communication of this kind of knowledge, which emerged out of new situations. A well-meaning critic called this book a modern book of comfort. This is high praise, but we do not want to forget that the comfort here takes its lonely course through reflections and meditations.

Santiago de Compostela
Summer 1958

NOTE This Foreword to the Spanish edition (*Ex captivitate salus: Experiencias de los años 1945–1946*, Santiago de Compostela 1960, translated by Anima Schmitt de Otero) was added by Carl Schmitt to both personal copies of the German edition of *Ex captivitate salus*, held in the estate of Carl Schmitt, State Archive of North Rhine-Westphalia, RW 265–21245 and 21479. In both cases there are two pages of typewritten carbon copies with handwritten corrections. A German version of the Foreword to the Spanish edition was first published on the basis of a reverse translation from the Spanish template of Günter Maschke in Schmittiana II, Brussels 1990, pp. 79–80.

Notes

Notes to Introduction

1 Chapter 6, p. 63.
2 For instance, see Carl Schmitt, "Wesen und Werden des faschistischen Staates" [1929], in idem, *Positionen und Begriffe im Kampf mit Weimar—Genf—Versailles, 1923–1939*, Berlin: Duncker & Humblot, 2014 [1940], pp. 109–15; Carl Schmitt, "Führertum als Grundbegriff des nationalsozialistischen Rechts," *Europäische Revue*, 9.11 (1933): 676–9; Carl Schmitt, "Nationalsozialismus und Rechtsstaat," *Juristische Wochenschrift*, 63.12/13 (1934): 713–8; Carl Schmitt, "Ein Jahr nationalsozialistischer Verfassungsstaat," *Deutsches Recht*, 4.2 (1934): 27–30; Carl Schmitt, "Nationalsozialistisches Rechtsdenken," *Deutsches Recht*, 4.10 (1934): 225–9; Carl Schmitt, "Die Rechtswissenschaft im Führerstaat," *Zeitschrift der Akademie für Deutsches Recht*, 2.7 (1935): 435–8; Carl Schmitt, "Faschistische und nationalsozialistische Rechtswissenschaft," *Deutsche Juristen-Zeitung*, 10 (1936): 619–20; Carl Schmitt, "Die nationalsozialistische Gesetzgebung und der Vorbehalt des 'ordre public' im internationalen Privatrecht," *Zeitschrift der Akademie für Deutsches Recht*, 3 (1936): 204–11; Carl Schmitt, "Die deutsche Rechtswissenschaft im Kampf gegen den jüdischen Geist," *Deutschen Juristen-Zeitung*, 41 (1936): 1193–9.

3 Carl Schmitt, "Interrogation by Robert Kempner (I–III)," *Telos: A Quarterly of Critical Thought*, 72 (1987): 97–107, at p. 106.

4 Renato Cristi, *Carl Schmitt and Authoritarian Liberalism*, Cardiff: University of Wales Press, 1998, p. 28.

5 Carl Schmitt, "Der Führer schützt das Recht: Zur Reichstagsrede Adolf Hitlers vom 13. Juli 1934," *Deutsche Juristen-Zeitung*, 39 (1934): 945–50.

6 Reinhard Mehring, *Carl Schmitt: A Biography*, trans. Daniel Steuer. Cambridge: Polity, 2014, p. 416; Carl Schmitt, *Glossarium: Aufzeichnungen der Jahre 1947–1951*. Berlin: Duncker & Humblot, 1991, p. 97 (entry dated February 13, 1948).

7 See chapter 1, pp. 14, 15; chapter 6, p. 63.

8 Jacob Taubes, "Carl Schmitt: Apocalyptic Prophet of the Counterrevolution," in idem, *To Carl Schmitt: Letters and Reflections*, trans. Keith Tribe with an introduction by Mike Grimshaw. New York: Columbia University Press, 2013, p. 1.

9 During his 1947 interrogation, Schmitt was questioned in relation to his *Grossraum* (great space) theory and German expansionist policy, his official participation in the decision-making structures of the party and the state, and his role in the Jewish Question. See Joseph W. Bendersky, *Carl Schmitt: Theorist for the Reich*. Princeton University Press, 1983, pp. 268–72; Joseph W. Bendersky, "Carl Schmitt at Nuremberg," *Telos*, 72 (1987): 91–6.

10 Chapter 1, p. 13.

11 Appendix, p. 76; see also the last paragraph in chapter 5, p. 62.

12 Chapter 5, p. 61. A few years later he will describe this tiny text as an "urgent cry," an "ultimate appeal" against the reigning silence in Germany: see Schmitt, *Glossarium*, pp. 310–1 (entry dated September 30, 1950). See also Jan-Werner Müller, *A Dangerous Mind: Carl Schmitt in Post-War European Thought*. New Haven, CT: Yale University Press, 2003, pp. 54, 59.

13 Gopal Balakrishnan, *The Enemy: An Intellectual Portrait of Carl Schmitt*. London: Verso, 2000, p. 257.

14 Carl Schmitt, *Dialogues on Power and Space*, ed. Andreas Kalyvas and Federico Finchelstein, trans. Samuel Garrett Zeitlin. Cambridge: Polity, 2015.

15 Chapter 1, p. 15.

16 Chapter 2, p. 21.

17 Chapter 2, p. 18.

18 Jacob Taubes, *The Political Theology of Paul*. Palo Alto, CA: Stanford University Press, 2003, p. 69; Taubes, *To Carl Schmitt*, p. 6.

19 The paradigmatic formulation is Carl Schmitt, *The Nomos of the Earth in the International Law of the jus publicum Europaeum*, trans. with commentary by G. L. Ulmen. New York: Telos Press, 2003, pp. 309–22.

20 Chapter 2, pp. 16–17.

21 Chapter 1, p. 15.

22 Chapter 5, p. 60; see also Schmitt, *Glossarium*, p. 229 (entry dated April 4, 1949).

23 Appendix, p. 75.

24 Appendix, p. 75.

25 Appendix, p. 75.

26 Seeing the world from the perspective of the defeated put him in league with many other defeated figures of the European intellectual tradition: Alexis de Tocqueville, Niccolò Machiavelli, Thomas Hobbes—even Benjamin Constant. Different parts of the book present a variety of moments of deep identification.

27 Schmitt, *The Nomos of the Earth*, pp. 217–19.

28 Carl Schmitt, "La tensión planetaria entre Oriente y Occidente y la oposición de Tierra y Mar," *Revista de Estudios Políticos*, 52 (1955): 3–28; Carl Schmitt, "Die weltgeschichtliche Struktur des heutigen Weltgegensatzes von Ost und West: Bemerkungen zu Ernst Jüngers Schrift 'Der gordische Knoten'" [1955], in idem, *Staat, Großraum, Nomos: Arbeiten aus den Jahren 1916–1969*, ed. Günter Maschke. Berlin: Duncker & Humblot, 1995, pp. 523–51; Carl Schmitt, "The New *nomos* of the Earth" [1950], in idem, *The Nomos of the Earth*, pp. 351–5.

29 Karl Jaspers, *The Question of German Guilt*, trans. E. B. Ashton. New York: Dial Press, 1947.

30 Carl Schmitt, "Die Ordnung der Welt nach dem Zweiten Weltkrieg" [1962], in idem, *Staat, Großraum, Nomos*, pp. 598, 597; Carl Schmitt, "Die Einheit der Welt" [1952], in idem, *Staat, Großraum, Nomos*, p. 500.

31 Carl Schmitt, "Gespräch über den Partisanen: Carl Schmitt und Joachim Schickel" [1969], in idem, *Staat, Großraum, Nomos*, p. 623.

32 Chapter 5, pp. 52, 53.

33 *The Nomos of the Earth* was written in the early 1940s, as was the essay "The Plight of European Jurisprudence" (an English version appeared in 1990, in *Telos*, 83: 35–70). The first drafts of the essay on Donoso Cortés were presented in 1944 at various international talks (an English version was published in 2002 in *Telos*, 125: 100–12).

34 Chapter 6, p. 72.

35 Schmitt, "Interrogation by Robert Kempner," p. 107.

Notes to Chapter 1

1 Translator's note: In Hebrew, the word for "the devil" or "Satan" comes from the same root as the word that means "prosecutor." The translator is grateful to the editors for this point.

Notes to Chapter 2

1 Translator's note: Schmitt here refers to a fictional animal whose existence was inferred by the legal scholar Philipp Eduard Huschke in his 1838 treatise *Die Verfassung des Königs Servius Tullius* (available online at https://archive.org/details/dieverfassungde00tullgoog), pp. 245ff, esp. at 248. On the basis of the principle that God had provided five categories of being in order to relieve humans of core forms of exertion in gaining sustenance, Huschke surmised that, alongside the bull, the horse, the mule, and the ass, there must exist a fifth type of animal: the bovigus, whose purpose was to drive the bull by pulling the plow, specifically with tusks.

2 Translator's note: Herman Melville (2000 [1855]), *Bartleby and Benito Cereno*. Mineola, NY: Dover Publications.
3 Translator's note: Ernst Junger (1983 [1939]), *On the Marble Cliffs*. New York: Penguin Books.
4 This did happen at the time and was no longer possible later.
5 Translator's note: *Verstehen*—which is a key concept for Mannheim.
6 Translator's note: Probably a reference to a passage from Georg W. F. Hegel (1977 [1807]), *Hegel's Phenomenology of Spirit*, trans. A. V. Miller. Oxford: Oxford University Press: Section BB.VI.B.II.a, "The struggle of the Enlightenment with superstition", pp. 329ff.

Notes to Chapter 3

1 Translator's note: Johannes Annegarn (1899), *Weltgeschichte in acht Bänden* [*World History in Eight Volumes*], 8th edn. Münster: Druck und Verlag der Theissing'chen Buchhandlung.
2 Translator's note: Since the other affiliations Schmitt lists here are national, *Ultramontanen* can likewise be translated in a political–geographical register, as "Italians." However, with the term *ultramontanes* he probably also wishes to signal that Catholic approaches to history were marginalized during this period.
3 Translator's note: Heraclitus (2008), *Fragments*, trans. B. Haxton. New York: Penguin Classics, p. 29. The Presocratic philosopher Heraclitus lived some time in the sixth–fifth century BC.
4 Translator's note: Alexis de Tocqueville (1987), *Recollections: The French Revolution of 1848*, trans. G. Lawrence. Piscataway, NJ: Transaction Publishers. The original work appeared around 1859.
5 Translator's note: Alexis de Tocqueville (2003), *Democracy in America*, 2 vols., trans. G. Bevan. New York: Penguin Classics.
6 Translator's note: Originally an important concept in ancient

Stoic ethics, *to katechon* ("that which restrains/withholds," hence "(moral) obligation," "what is due"; neuter participle from the verb *katechein*, "to hold fast, contain") was taken up by the Christian eschatological tradition and is discussed by Schmitt in a number of contexts. In the masculine, *ho katechōn* ("the one who restrains") is a restraining figure or a force that prevents the Anti-Christ from appearing fully in the world, because that appearance must first take place before the arrival of Judgment Day. The translator is grateful to Rory Rowan for clarification of the (modern) Christian history of this ancient term.

Notes to Chapter 4

1 Translator's note: In German this sentence rhymes: *Die slawische Geduld wird Herrin unserer Schuld.*

2 Translator's note: Heinrich von Kleist (1989 [1810]), *On a Theatre of Marionettes*, trans. G. Wilford. London: Acorn Press.

3 Translator's note: Heinrich von Kleist (2002 [1811]), *The Prince of Homburg*, trans. N. Bartlett. London: Oberon Books.

4 Translator's note: Here Schmitt follows Däubler in preserving the referential ambiguity of *Heiden* as both "of the heaths," which accords with the plant theme in Däubler's poem "Grünes Elysium" ["Green Elysium"], and "of the heathen," which suggests the late Roman identification of Germanic tribes as heathens and resonates with Schmitt's portrayal of German cultural history in terms of East versus West. This line is translated by Jacques de Ville as "The plants teach us the sweet heathen/heaths dying": see Jacques de Ville (2016), "Schmitt's *Weisheit der Zelle*: Rethinking the Concept of the Political," in *Law, Memory and Violence: Uncovering the Counter-Archive*, ed. Stewart Motha and Honni von Rijswijk. Abingdon: Routledge, p. 224, n. 28. Kleist's poem "Grünes Elysium" is available in German at http://www.gedichte.eu/ex/daeubler/das-sternenkind/gruenes-elysium.php.

5 Translator's note: Possibly a reference to the Greek mythical figure Euphorion, son of Achilles and Helen of Troy, who was killed by Zeus with a thunderbolt.

6 Translator's note: Schmitt is probably referring here to one of the pieces in Annette von Droste-Hülshoff (1992 [1851]), *Das geistliche Jahr und religiöse Dichtungen* [*The Spiritual Year and Religious Poems*]. Vaduz: Liechtenstein Verlag. The full German text is available online at http://gutenberg.spiegel.de/buch/das-geistliche-jahr-2840/1.

7 Translator's note: Theodor Däubler (2013 [1910]), *Das Nordlicht* (Florentiner Ausgabe) [*Northern Lights* (Florence edition)]. N.p.: CreateSpace Independent Publishing Platform. Carl Schmitt published a separate study of Däubler's epic: Carl Schmitt (1991 [1916]), *Theodor Däublers "Nordlicht": Drei Studien über die Elemente, den Geist und die Aktualität des Werkes* [*Theodor Däubler's "Northern Lights": Three Studies on the Elements, the Spirit and the Topicality of the Work*]. Berlin: Duncker & Humblot.

8 Translator's note: *Der Wandrer will sich zu Wartenden legen*—a line from Däubler's poem "Oh Nacht, oh unendliche, herrliche Nacht" ("Oh Night, oh Endless, Magnificent Night"). The full German text is available online at http://gedichte.xbib.de/D%E4ubler_gedicht_538.+Oh+Nacht,+oh+unendliche,+herrliche+Nacht.htm.

9 Translator's note: From Däubler, *Northern Lights* (see n. 7).

10 Translator's note: From Theodor Däubler (1985 [1915]), "Der Nachtwandler," in Theodor Däubler, *Der Sternhelle Weg* [*The Starlit Way*], ed. Harald Kass. Munich: Carl Hanser Verlag. The full German text is available online at http://www.gedichte.eu/ex/daeubler/der-sternehelle-weg/der-nachtwandler.php. Schmitt here misquotes the line in one particular. The original line is *Alles klingt zu eines Balles Unversuchtem Rundungstraum*, but Schmitt substitutes *wird* (becomes) for *klingt* (sounds or chimes).

11 Translator's note: For a sense of what Schmitt has in mind in this unusual formulation, compare the sculpture of the River Nile in the Vatican Museums. Image available online at

http://www.gettyimages.com/detail/news-photo/old-father-
nile-ancient-roman-sculpture-also-known-as-news-photo/
463968585?#old-father-nile-ancient-roman-sculpture-also-
known-as-colossus-of-the-picture-id463968585.

12 Translator's note: Schmitt, *Theodor Däublers "Nordlicht"* (see
    n. 7).

13 Translator's note: Pierre-Joseph Proudhon (2015 [1865]),
    Du principe de l'art et de sa destination sociale [*On the
    Principle of Art and Its Social Destination*]. Delhi: Facsimile
    Publisher.

14 Translator's note: Johann Jakob Bachofen (1973 [1861]), *Myth,
    Religion and Mother Right: Selected Writings of J. J. Bachofen*,
    trans. R. Manheim. Princeton, NJ: Princeton University Press.
    Bachofen relies heavily on Plutarch throughout his writings on
    mythology.

15 Translator's note: Konrad Weiß (1921), *Die Cumäische Sybille*
    [*The Sybil of Cumae*]. Munich: Georg Müller Verlag. The full
    German text is available online at http://www.seiten-der-
    dichtung.de/konradweiss/dcs/toc.html. Konrad Weiß (1929).
    Tantalus. Augsburg: Dr. Benno Filser Verlag. The full German
    text is available online at http://www.seiten-der-dichtung.de/
    konradweiss/tantalus.html. Konrad Weiß (1933), *Der christ-
    liche Epimetheus* [*The Christian Epimetheus*]. Berlin: Edwin
    Runge. The full German text is available online at http://www.
    seiten-der-dichtung.de/konradweiss/dce.html.

16 Translator's note: Konrad Weiß, *Tantalus* (see n. 16).

Notes to Chapter 5

1 Translator's note: If *Jurisdiktion* were translated in the everyday
   sense of "jurisdiction," the sentence would lack clear meaning.
   What is submitted to in civil war is not the jurisdiction of the
   enemy—quite the opposite: each side attempts to force the
   enemy to submit to its own jurisdiction. Here Schmitt means
   Juris-Diktion rather etymologically, as *Rechts-Sprechung*.
   "Submission" to the jurisprudence of the enemy thus means
   submission to a form of legal thinking premised on the friend–

enemy distinction so central to Schmitt's agonistic conception of politics.

2 Translator's note: Both italicized words appear in English in the original text.

3 Translator's note: Attributed to Konrad Weiß by Linjing Jiang (2013), *Carl Schmitt als Literaturkritiker: Eine Metakritische Untersuchung* [*Carl Schmitt as Literary Critic: A Metacritical Investigation*]. PhD diss., Heidelberg University (http://archiv. ub.uni-heidelberg.de/volltextserver/15770/1/Dissertation. pdf), p. 140. The verse echoes text in the libretto of Christoph Willibald Gluck's opera *Orpheus und Eurydike* [*Orpheus and Eurydice*], premiered in 1762.

4 Translator's note: *Schur* means "clipping" or "shearing," as of sheep. Schmitt seems basically to mean here that, like Jesus on the cross, we establish a connection to God when we cry out in the extremity of suffering. Why he uses the imagery of shearing to express this is unclear.

5 Translator's note: The English word *camp* appears in the original.

6 Translator's note: The words *amity line* are in English in the original.

7 Translator's note: The call is repeated at the end of a number of chapters of Gentili's writings on just war. See Alberico Gentili (1995 [1589]), *Three Books on the Law of War*. Buffalo, NY: William S. Hein.

8 Translator's note: John of Salisbury (1991), *Policraticus*. Cambridge: Cambridge University Press. The work was originally produced around the mid-twelfth century.

9 Translator's note: Benjamin Constant (1980 [1816]), *Adolphe*, trans. Alexander Walker. London: Penguin Books.

10 Translator's note: Ernst Jünger (1983 [1939]), *On the Marble Cliffs*. New York: Penguin Books.

Notes to Chapter 6

1 Translator's note: Theodor Däubler, "Perseus," in idem, *Der sternenhelle Weg* [*The Starlit Way*], ed. Harald Kass. Munich:

Carl Hanser Verlag (available online at http://www.gedichte.
eu/ex/daeubler/der-sternehelle-weg/der-nachtwandler.php).

2 Translator's note: Richard Wagner (1985 [1876]), *Twilight of
the Gods* [*Götterdämmerung*], trans. A. Porter. London: Calder
Publishers, Act I, Scene 1, line 2. This translation of the
opera's text can be found at http://www.rwagner.net/libretti/
gotterd/e-gott-a1s2.html.

3 Translator's note: Stefan Pegatzky suggests that the line from
Wagner's opera paraphrases a passage from Max Stirner;
see Stefan Pegatzky (2002), *Das poröse Ich: Leiblichkeit und
Aesthetik von Arthur Schopenhauer zu Thomas Mann* [*The Porous
I: Corporality and Aesthetics from Arthur Schopenhauer to Thomas
Mann*]. Würzburg: Königshausen und Neumann, p. 188, n.
425. See also Max Stirner (2016 [1844]), *The Ego and Its Own*.
N.p.: CreateSpace Independent Publishing Platform, p. 257.

4 Translator's note: Pennalism denotes a hierarchical relation
of service between newly matriculated and older members of
regional student fraternities (*Landsmannschaften*), largely at
Protestant universities, especially in the sixteenth and seventeenth centuries.

5 Translator's note: See above, n. 3.

6 Translator's note: *The Garden of Earthly Delights* is the title
later given to a triptych painted by Hieronymous Bosch
between 1490 and 1510, which is now housed at the Prado in
Madrid.

7 Translator's note: This is a reference to the eponymous character in Gioacchino Rossini's opera *La gazza ladra* (*The Thieving
Magpie*), first performed in Milan in 1817.

8 Translator's note: "Earth-conscious" [*erdbewußt*] is an allu-
sion to Däubler's *Northern Lights*, which contains lines such as
"Die alle Erdenbrunst in das Bewußtsein leitet." See Theodor
Däubler (2013 [1910]), *Das Nordlicht* (Florentiner Ausgabe).
N.p.: CreateSpace Independent Publishing Platform. The full
text of this epic poem is available at http://gutenberg.spiegel.
de/buch/das-nordlicht-2075/1 (Text im Projekt Gutenberg).

9 Translator's note: Virgil (2009), *The Eclogues and the Georgics*,
trans. C. Day Lewis. Oxford: Oxford Classics, p. 19. The

Fourth Eclogue is famous for the interpretations it had gener-
ated over the identity of its subject—a savior and future ruler
of the world, whose birth this poem celebrates.

10 Translator's note: Aldous Huxley (2007 [1932]), *Brave New
World*. New York: Vintage.

11 Translator's note: From Theodor Däubler (1916), *Hymne an
Italien* [*Hymn to Italy*]. Munich: Georg Müller.

12 Translator's note: Paraphrase of a line from the opening
stanzas of Konrad Weiß's *The Christian Epimetheus*. The translation above, "from which meaning springs by right," is at
odds with that given by Jacques de Ville: "upon which the law
of meaning grows"; see Jacques de Ville (2016), "Schmitt's
Weisheit der Zelle: Rethinking the Concept of the Political,"
in *Law, Memory and Violence: Uncovering the Counter-Archive*,
ed. Stewart Motha and Honni von Rijswijk. Abingdon:
Routledge, p. 228. De Ville's translation, probably suggested
by word order, runs against the syntax of cases (*dem Recht*,
dative and *der Sinn*, nominative).

13 Translator's note: Konrad Weiß (1933), *Der christliche
Epimetheus*. Berlin: Edwin Runge (available at http://www.
seiten-der-dichtung.de/konradweiss/dce.html).

Notes to Chapter 7

1 Translator's note: The French *escavessade* refers to a bitless
halter called a cavesson, used in equine dressage. *Escavessade*
is the use of this halter to steer or rein in a horse. Schmitt
seems to want to evoke here the historical events' effect of
unexpectedly pulling our attention and activities in always new
directions. See Johann Zedler (ed.) (1995–9), *Großes, vollstän-
diges Universallexikon aller Wissenschaften und Künste* [*The Large,
Complete Universal Lexicon of all Sciences and Arts*], 2nd reprint
of the Halle/Leipzig edition (first published between 1732 and
1751–4). Graz: Akademische Drück- und Verlagsanstalt, vol.
8, col. 1855.

2 Translator's note: A vesper hymn for the dead in the Catholic
tradition.

Notes to Appendix

1 Translator's note: Silvio Pellico (2010 [1847]), *Le mie prigioni* [*My Prisons*]. Whitefish, MT: Kessinger Publishing.
2 Translator's note: Paul Verlaine (2003 [1904]), *Mes prisons* [*My Prisons*]. Paris: Mille et une nuits.
3 Translator's note: Oscar Wilde (2010 [1898]), *The Ballad of Reading Gaol and Other Poems*. London: Penguin Classics.

Index